MUSICAL TASTE AND HOW TO FORM IT

MUSICAL TASTE AND HOW TO FORM IT

By

M. D. CALVOCORESSI

OXFORD UNIVERSITY PRESS
LONDON: HUMPHREY MILFORD
1925

Printed in England at
The Westminster Press, 411a Harrow Road
London, W.9

TO THE DEAR MEMORY OF
HENRY BEVAN

INTRODUCTORY NOTE

T H E idea of writing a book on Musical Taste occurred to me many years ago. But it was only while writing my book *Principles and Methods of Musical Criticism* that I saw how I could do it in the way I wished ; and only after bringing out and demonstrating to the best of my ability, in the said book, certain fundamental principles that I felt it possible to simplify my statement of the same principles for the purposes of the general music-loving public—occasionally referring readers to the fuller comments provided in my book for more advanced readers.

There will be little difficulty in pointing out that whereas I criticize and contradict the notions and suggestions of other authors freely, my own suggestions are, all told, very similar. Let it be explained, therefore, that as a rule it is not with what other authors recommend that I have a quarrel, but with certain reasons they give for recommending it— which reasons, I fear, will often lead to incorrect focussing and to misapprehension of these principles' purport. When I contradict, it is not with the ambition of proving myself right at anybody else's expense, but with the hope of assisting a little towards the discovery of the sound method of musical education which all of us writers on Taste and Appreciation are intent upon establishing.

Chelsea, *July* 1924   M. D. C.

CONTENTS

CHAPTER I

THE CASE FOR ADVICE

T H E question is often asked, why should I learn to enjoy music? Now I, who am writing this book, may safely assume that there is no need for me to fight the matter out with you from the beginning : for if you did not wish to know something of music and of the education of musical taste, you would never dream of opening this book.

But you may have various reasons for reading it. Perhaps, enjoying music already, you feel that you might enjoy it more keenly, or enjoy a greater variety of it, or that there is more in it to enjoy that you actually are aware of. My reply will be : yes, you might, and there is. All of us could enjoy music more than we do, and find more in it than we find, and learn to enjoy a greater variety of it than we enjoy. Whoever has tasted the delights of music will realize what this prospect means, and feel that any trouble he takes to study music and to remain in intimate contact with it will be repaid a thousandfold and more.

This is equally true with regard to people who at first were indifferent to music, or even disliked it. Mr. J. D. M. Rorke, in his book *A Musical Pilgrim's Progress*, and Dr. Agnes Savill, in *Music, Health, and Character*, tell us how, having chanced to hear music that appealed to them, they were led to discover in themselves and to develop a fondness for music of which they had long remained altogether unaware. *A Musical Pilgrim's Progress* is a grand and attractive little book, which I advise you to peruse as soon as possible. It is published by the Oxford University Press.

Perhaps you have not yet felt attracted by music, but you know how great a boon music is to others, and wish to have your share in this boon. Or, maybe, feeling that music is a great joy to you, you are unwilling to admit that by learning more about it, by going out of your way to follow other people's advice, you will increase your joy: you will have opened this book merely to find fresh confirmation of these views of yours. You have no patience with all those fellows who volunteer to help you improve your taste, and you are convinced that they can teach you nothing worth a plain music-lover's while.

But even if you mistrust advice, you know that in all things which interest you, what you seek is a greater experience and variety of experiences. Suppose your hobby to be carpentry, you would derive scant enjoyment from turning out the same type of bracket again and again. If you are fond of walking, you hardly wish to take the same walk every day. Well, there you have it all in a nutshell: what you need is to know more music; and this, in turn, is the only way to know more about music. Music, just as it stands, contains everything there is to know about music. Nothing but music will teach you music's secrets.

Yet, since so many people proffer help by writing books and articles on music, you may be tempted to avail yourself of their assistance. But not necessarily: neither Mr. Rorke nor Dr. Savill seems to have sought much help in writings on music. I, on the other hand, began to read books on music and musical journals as soon as I began to feel attracted by music, because I felt that besides wanting to hear music, I wanted to know things about music. I likewise felt that there was much to learn from other people's musical experiences and study of music. In due course, I learnt to take nothing on trust, not even praise or blame emanating from the writers whom I considered soundest and most sensitive and thoughtful; for I encountered a bewildering discrepancy of views. Here were two authors who agreed in their appraisement of Beethoven and Wagner but disagreed in their appraisement of Berlioz; another two agreed on Beethoven, Wagner, and Berlioz, but disagreed on Liszt;

others, agreeing on Beethoven, Wagner, Liszt, and Berlioz, would disagree on Strauss or Hugo Wolf, and so on. Books written on the philosophy of music, or on what has since been called Musical Appreciation, struck me as even more bewildering on account of the contradictions I encountered in them, and of their lack of convincingness.

A beginner reading books on music and criticisms of music will soon find himself at sea, especially if he reads things written about contemporary music. So long as you stick to one writer whose assertions do not go against your grain, all will appear simple and clear enough—so simple and clear, in fact, that there is a danger of your forming the impression that no other opinion can exist. If your readings include many authors, you will find that when one says black another says white, a third gives you a chequered pattern, a fourth favours a non-committal shade of grey. In proportion as you read more, you will encounter all the shades of the rainbow. The only composers whose works are praised by all sensible and expert judges are the great classics.

The word ' classic ' is used in two senses : as opposed to ' modern', and as opposed to ' romantic.' Some people, stretching a point, use it to mean sensible, clear, and balanced, as opposed to extravagant, complicated, and maundering. The first meaning alone concerns us here.

The classics, then, are composers whose works have survived because generation after generation of music lovers tried them and found them good, irrespective of passing fashions and even of particularities of race and period. The fact that their works delight music lovers of one century as much as they delighted those of another proves these works to possess vitality, the supreme merit of a work of art.

Contemporary works are untested, nor do people agree about their merits. But should you come across old books and periodicals, you will see how very often professional

critics misjudged the very works which posterity has found
most admirable : Beethoven's or Wagner's, for instance.
You will see that their strictures on Beethoven's or Wagner's
music are often couched in the very same words as strictures
passed by other professional critics on the works of modern
composers ; and this will probably confirm you in your
resolve to take nothing for granted.

In order to speed this confirmation, my first piece of
advice to you is : if you read, read more than one author.
Read as many as you can in reason. The more you read, the
better your chance of encountering the very sayings that
are needful, the sayings that will shed light on your instinctive feelings and stimulate them—which is the only practical
object of criticism. Read conflicting judgements. Do not let
them bewilder you. Take them for what they are : so many
warnings against all forms of rash judgement. Let them inspire you with the desire to decide for yourself, by hearing
the music to which they refer.

I do not insist on your reading books and articles on
music before you start with the music itself. And whether
you do so before or after, one question arises : is it likely
that where experienced judges differ on modern works, you
will always be able to make up your mind, and always be
right when you do ? The reply being ' probably not ', you
may incline to wonder why, since between the music that
appeals to your own instinctive taste and the music on whose
merits all the best judges agree there is more than enough
to provide for a life-time's enjoyment, you should wish or
should be asked to trouble about contemporary works upon
which doubt may exist.

There are several reasons. One is that if great artists live
in your time, you owe it to yourself and to them to acknowledge them. It is not right that their merits should go un-
rewarded. It is essentially a question of fair play. But I wish
to appeal to your more selfish instincts as well. If things
worth enjoying exist, you naturally wish to enjoy them.

Remember that the classics of to-day were 'modern' in their time, and 'modern' (or progressive) in their tendencies as well as in bare point of dates. If not, they would never have become classics, because they would have been mere imitators of the past, who repeated but did not create. If you enjoy Beethoven or Wagner or Schumann to-day, it should be enough to make you feel how desirable it would have been to enjoy them had you lived in their times. So that for your own sake, as well as for the sake of the artists who devote their life to creating fine music, it is essential that you should be prepared to appreciate to-day's music as well as yesterday's, and as much of it as is compatible with your own nature and the enlightenment which experience brings.

CHAPTER II

THE ADVISER'S QUANDARY

A WHILE ago, I referred to contradictory statements on music. You must be prepared to encounter contradictions not only in writings in which musical works are judged, but in writings on musical aesthetics and theory, and even in writings on appreciation and on the forming of musical taste. In this book, I contradict a good many things set forth by writers who have devoted much thought and labour to devising schemes for helping and educating music lovers. I am fully aware of it, and have not done so without due consideration.

I happen to be convinced that certain courses recommended by these authors are beset with pitfalls or lead to blind alleys; and I am trying to suggest a safer course. This course, I fear, may seem at first less secure, because I shall lay down no rules, and give no recipe for deciding which music is good and which is bad. If you are genuinely interested in music, and apply my first bit of advice, you will not be guided by me only, but will read several books on musical taste besides this one : so you will be able to decide for yourselves whether the line I suggest will suit your requirements best or not.

The beauty of music is altogether inexplicable. It is possible to lay down a few general principles—Sir Henry Hadow has done it admirably in the first chapter of his *Studies in Modern Music* (two volumes, Seely and Co.), which you will read with great profit ; but as soon as an attempt is made to define their application, the ground is no longer safe.

The task of giving practical advice regarding the appraisement of music and education of taste is so exceedingly hard that most writers, in despair of finding the straight way, resort to roundabout ways. The main point is elusive: so they naturally cast about for some definite, concrete foundation, which they generally find in theoretical, historical, and biographical considerations. Theoretical analyses and explanations are particularly tempting, because they seem so very much to the point and difficult to contradict. Author after author will warn his readers, very rightly, that the theoretical understanding of music has nothing to do with the ability to understand it as a language of the emotions and imagination, and immediately afterwards proceed to establish all his assertions as regards musical beauty on a theoretical basis of some kind. And you will presently find me, too, talking theory to you.

But my excuse is that I shall try to take every precaution in order to avoid misleading you about the value of theoretical considerations, and to make it clear—perhaps rather monotonously—that they never provide a standard or proof of beauty.

The truth is, however, that it is impossible to talk music without talking technique or theory. Can you imagine anyone talking of painting, and never using such words as colour, design, red, blue, curve, light, shadow, foreground, and so forth? or of poetry, and never alluding to rhythm or style or vocabulary? Talking music, we cannot avoid using terms that refer to the materials and conditions of music. When we say how wonderful the tone of the horns is at the beginning of Weber's *Freyschütz* Overture, or the ethereal notes of the violins at the beginning of Wagner's *Lohengrin* Prelude, or how interested we were, after hearing some tune or motive at the beginning of a piece of music, to hear it again in the course or at the close of that piece, informed with new significance by virtue of certain changes in tone, character, or surroundings, we are talking technique. And there is no other relevant way of singling out the beauties in a piece of music.

Hence the temptation, for writers on appreciation, to mingle technical disquisitions with disquisitions on the interest and beauty of music. It is just as if Mr. Arnold Bennett had tried to compress into his excellent little book *Literary Taste and How to Form It* a grammar, a dictionary, a course in memory training, and a good many other things. The result, of course, is that you get far too little of any one thing to be of real use, and you never know exactly where you stand.

If your interest in music is genuine, you will surely wish to know a few elementary things about music as a first step towards greater and more helpful knowledge. Theoretical knowledge *is* helpful up to a certain point.

One important reason why books on musical appreciation differ from books on the appreciation of the other arts is because it is possible to admit that everybody knows something about the materials used by literature—words—and by the fine arts—lines, shapes, and colours—and about the topics and subjects with which all these arts deal. But not everybody knows something about the materials and content of music.

For instance, Mr. Arnold Bennett, in his *Literary Taste* (this little book, published by the New Age Press, has greatly helped me in planning and writing this one, and I strongly recommend your reading it : for the greater part of his advice is as useful towards forming musical taste as it is toward forming literary taste), is able to start without bothering to tell his readers all about words and the use of words and facts and ideas. He rightly assumed that they knew at least the essentials without which they would find literature a sealed book.

Now music consists of sounds, exactly as literature of words and paintings of lines, shapes, and colours. In order to enjoy music you must be capable, first, of perceiving the subtlest differences between sounds and sounds and between various patterns in sounds ; and secondly, of following the course of the music you hear. If you cannot do the former, music will mean no more to you than a picture would to a man incapable of telling red from blue or a straight line from a curve. If you cannot do the latter you will be in the same undesirable position as a man who forgets each word of a sentence in proportion as he hears the following word. Hence, being a music lover, actual or potential, your first object is to train your ear and memory.

To both these ends theory helps by providing certain lines along which to proceed, and a nomenclature that enables us to reduce our impressions and memories to some sort of order. All this, of course, is essential. Whether these two faculties, keenness of ear and retentiveness of memory, need be conscious or not is a disputed point ; but what remains sure is that if you are to train your ear and memory it must be by conscious exercise: and this again means the use of a system of names.

Let it be clear that it is not the capacity to label and docket and pigeon-hole that matters, because nothing which you can label and docket and pigeon-hole provides a standard or a proof of musical beauty. This is the second time I use these words, and in the course of the book I shall probably repeat the warning more than once so as to make sure that it will sink in.

Theoretical explanations and technical analyses will bring you no nearer to the principles of musical beauty than anatomy to the principle of life. But any method of approach is good so far as it brings you into close contact with music, compels your attention, and sows the seeds of perseverance.

As soon as you realize how very useful technical knowledge is, provided it is made neither an idol nor a bogy, you will begin to long for the assistance it affords. You will eventually wish to know far more than is to be found in any one handbook, because you are bound to realize sooner or later that a mere smattering is of no real avail.

I suggest that you defer the actual study of theory until

that moment comes. Meanwhile, any good, simple primer will provide you with the mere names you may need at the outset. The more plainly it is a primer of musical theory and not a mixture of theoretical information and advice on appreciation, used as props for one another, the better it will suit the purpose for which I advise its use. Good ones are Franklin Peterson's *Introduction to the Study of Theory* and *Catechism of Music* and Prof. Niecks's *Introduction to the Elements of Music*—all three are published by Augener, London.

CHAPTER III

WHERE TO START

SUBSTITUTING the word music for the word literature, I copy Bennett's golden advice to beginners :

' When you have actually felt some of the emotions which
great composers have striven to impart to you, and when
your emotions become so numerous and puzzling that you
feel the need of arranging them and calling them by names,
then—and not before—you can begin to study what has been
attempted in the way of classifying and ticketing music.
You can only acquire really useful general ideas by first
acquiring particular ideas and putting those particular ideas
together. You cannot make bricks without straw. Do not
worry about music in the abstract, about theories as to
music. Get at it. Get hold of music in the concrete, as a dog
gets hold of a bone. It doesn't matter in the slightest degree
where you begin. Begin where the fancy takes you to begin.
Music is a whole.'

Bennett adds the following restriction : ' You must begin
with a classic, for the excellent reason that you are not in a
position to choose with certainty among modern works.
Your taste must pass before the bar of the classics.' The reasons
he gives (I advise you to read chapters I, IV, VII, and X of
his book at the very earliest opportunity) are excellent. Yet,
while granting that the same course would be highly desirable for you—the ideal, in my mind, would be to start with
the greatest of all classics, J. S. Bach—I do not incline to be
so emphatic on the point.

To me the main thing is that you should start with music
to which you readily respond. Remember that between our
enjoyment of music and our enjoyment of any other art,
there is this essential difference that everyday life contains

much that prepares us to enjoy the latter, but as a rule very little that directly prepares us to enjoy the former We have had emotions or even perhaps adventures similar to those with which literature deals ; we have the common objects of the world, we have speech, we have seen colours and shapes, scenery, and living beings. Even before we happen to see our first picture or to read our first piece of literature, we are, in a way, prepared for it. Not so with music. Unless we are born and live surrounded by it, at first it comes to us as a surprise, even if we feel that it corresponds to an innermost longing of ours.

Again, we are all accustomed to expressing ourselves in words, and occasionally at least to referring to our experiences and feelings in ways which, as Bennett points out, constitute the first germs of literature. Many of us have tried our hand at sketching. But how many ever express themselves spontaneously in music, except perhaps by humming some remembered or half-remembered tune ?

In spite of this, music must come to have as direct a significance for you as pictures or poems. This significance you must feel; and it is when you begin to feel it that the education of your taste starts. Nobody can help you to feel it, as Bennett helps you to feel the significance of an example of literature, by referring it to experiences of your own life.

There is a relation between music and the experiences of life (otherwise music would not have come into being), but only those experiences which are wholly within the composer's mind and soul—and, so far as you, the listener, are concerned, within *your* mind and soul. Joy, despair, elation, and countless other things, inspire composers : and their music makes you feel joyful or despairing or elated, speaking to you of many things. But it does not do so by telling you anything that might be told in words or represented in shapes and lines and colours. Its object is not to make you think of love, joy, despair; nor does it actually reckon with your previous experience of these feelings. Music must explain itself or remain unexplained and inexplicable. You must listen to its own voice, and find within your own self the key to the language it speaks.

Not a few advisers discourage beginners by laying down a certain course, including one classic after another, and perhaps mislead them as well by conveying the impression that modern music is best judged according to its degree of outward conformity to that of the classics. To me, whose sole concern is that you should love music and feel at home within it, it does not matter two pins where you start. I do not want you to love the classics out of a sense of duty, or to pretend to yourself that you love them when you do not.

But, you will ask, what if you start with the very music which is the least likely to contribute to the education of your taste? And how are you to tell which will contribute to it, and which will not?

You will find suggestions on these points in the chapters on Taste and Experience. Meanwhile let me tell you that the first requisite is to start with something that inspires you with a strong preference.

Artistic taste is entirely founded on the capacity to draw distinctions, to prefer certain things to certain others. Let us imagine a human being with a natural disposition for music who has never heard any in his life. The first music he hears, good or bad, will fly straight to his heart. Later, hearing more music, he will begin to know what he prefers and why. The more sharply he differentiates between the various examples of music he hears, the more surely his taste will progress. If you have the makings of a true music lover, there will surely be things which you prefer to others—which tell you something yet untold or open new vistas. This is the raw material you have to work on. So I begin by taking your taste as it stands, and only ask you to look out for some preference of this kind.

It is essential that this preference should be lasting. However attractive unworthy things may appear at first, their

attractiveness soon wears out. Think of all the magazine stories you found exciting when first you read them, but which you would not dream of reading again any more than your sister or wife would dream of wearing the fashions of the year before last. It is the same with music : you hear a drawing-room ballad or dance tune and like it, but soon after a new ballad or tune comes into fashion, and makes you forget all about the other ones, and you never wish to hear them again. But exactly as you can enjoy Shakespeare and Dickens and Tennyson over and over again if you enjoy them at all, so is it with music really worthy of being enjoyed.

Be sure I am as interested as you are to guide you towards the right kind of music. But I cannot actually help you to find out whence the spark will come that will kindle your love for music. If from a classic, all will go well with you, and you may trust that the attraction will prove lasting.

If from a modern composer, you are not quite so safe. So long as his music sounds in most respects similar to that of the classics, your main chance of going wrong is that you may now and then mistake a worthless imitation for the genuine thing. But if so, in proportion as you get acquainted with the actual classics, you will learn to feel what rings true and what does not. I should like you, of course, to save time and labour by starting with the actual classics rather than with their imitators.

It is when new music sounds utterly unlike anything heard before that caution is most necessary. To write music of this kind is as easy for a composer as it is for anybody to appear unlike other people by turning his coat inside out or dyeing his hair green. But on the other hand, remember that the music of the great classics was often described in its time as sounding utterly unlike anything heard before. All this, you realize, means that in itself strangeness (or the appearance of strangeness) is no indication of merit or demerit.

It is seldom easy to discriminate between novelty that is the outcome of genuine inspiration, and so valuable, and novelty that is not. Some people find it difficult to achieve any kind of discrimination between contemporary works that are at all unusual in style. It is all a matter of experience when it is not one of intuition. Likewise, some people appear incapable of seeing the difference between the classics and their imitators.

Until you are capable of subtle discrimination, you cannot of course progress very far. But if your intuition draws you towards a certain kind of unwonted music, follow it unhesitatingly. Perhaps your intuition is as right as was that of the first people who admired Beethoven or Wagner. Anyhow, it is right so far as your present purpose is concerned.

As you become familiar with music that attracts you, study yourself. Ask yourself what you are getting out of it, how it moves you, and why. Seek similar experiences in other works—this time, in the music of the classics if you started with modern music, or in modern music if you started with a classic. Take, if you can, an interest in both as soon as possible, lest you develop the habit of thinking or feeling that only the one or the other is best—a habit that is widespread and pernicious. I have already given you reasons why you should take an early interest in modern music, and here is another one : when you attend concerts, you have to take the programmes as they are ; and if a programme comprises a fine modern work (which perhaps you will have no other opportunity of hearing for months or even years) it would be a thousand pities for you not to be as capable of enjoying it as you are of enjoying the classical items.

If it is with a modern composer you start (I have actually known people who first learnt to love music through hearing Debussy at a time when Debussy's music was freely described as uncouth and senseless), make sure that he is an object of discussion among people interested in music. If all agree that his music is worthless, however much it may appeal to you, it may be safer for you to seek another starting-point until the moment comes when you will be able to form an enlightened judgement. But if you find that his works provide food for argument among reasonably experienced and unprejudiced judges, do not allow yourself to be deterred from following your inclination. Judging from what happened in the past, we may feel certain, as Mr. Edwin Evans has remarked, that any composer of to-day who will endure and become a classic belongs to the number of those whose music provokes heated discussions, not those who are accepted as a matter of course.

There is one point on which I must lay down a law as stern and emphatic as Bennett's ' begin with a classic.' For many reasons, but chiefly because I wish you to learn to enjoy music for its own sake, apart from the associations and other clues that words may suggest (I shall explain this more fully in the chapter *The Taste for The Music*), I urge you to begin with instrumental music, not with songs or operas. I do not mean that you are to avoid listening to songs or operas, but that you should, for the time being, base your scheme of taste-education upon instrumental works only. Devote the whole of your attention to works that will accustom you to hear, think, and feel music, not to works that will draw your attention, perhaps, to dramatic and sentimental points rather than towards music alone. You will thereby learn to appreciate song and opera all the better, whereas you might (as happens to many people) devote a whole life-time to song and opera without ever coming any nearer the power to enjoy a string quartet, or a symphony, or even lovely choral works such as the Tudor madrigals and the church music of Palestrina, whose scheme and appeal, broadly speaking, are altogether those of pure music.

There is one exception, and one only, that I incline to make. If your taste points that way, you may safely start with the works of Wagner's maturity—especially the *Ring*, *Tristan and Isolda*, and *The Mastersingers*. All these contain

a wonderful wealth of admirable music, and music of a kind well suited to train, under most attractive conditions, your ear and memory, while inducing your mind to elasticity.

In the *Ring* especially, the music is built out of a number of motives or small patterns, tunes, or just harmonies or rhythms, mostly interrelated, which appear and reappear, are developed and combined according to the suggestions and requirements of the text. To listen and realize the adventures of those motives or themes in the infinite variety of aspects they assume is capital and delightful practice, very similar to that provided by listening to a fine symphony, or fugue, or chamber work. I assume, of course, that you will be interested in all this because you feel the result to be beautiful music; the time for you to study a work in the hope of finding it beautiful has not yet come. And I hope that you will not be led to think that because Wagner's music contains leit-motives (as they are usually called), it is more beautiful than the music of Mozart's operas, which contains none.

But if you are not particularly drawn towards Wagner, begin with orchestral or chamber music. Piano and organ music are the next best things. Begin where you like within this range. Rest assured that if you are intended to become a true music lover, you will soon learn to feel at home with most of the great classics, and probably with all of them.

The finest music, classical or modern, is not more "difficult" than the most commonplace. For it is upon feeling and imagination, not upon any act of reasoning and analysing, that the comprehension of music depends. But you do not give your sensitiveness and imagination a fair chance if you do not listen intently and wholeheartedly. The chief object of wise advisers is to warn you against listening casually or half-heartedly.

CHAPTER IV

HOW TO START AND CONTINUE

T H E first question is, do you play or sing ? If so, you probably know something of the grammar of music—that is, so long as you have studied staff notation and not only tonic sol-fa—and your ear and memory may be trained to a degree. If not—and I am writing this book in the hope that it will prove intelligible and helpful even to those of you who do not play or sing, and who even know no theory—in proportion as your interest in music grows, you will wish to know more not only about music, but about the art and craft of music making.

So long as you cannot read and play music, your position will remain as unsatisfactory as that of a lover of literature who could not read, and depended entirely upon the chance of hearing other people read, act, or recite. You may derive great joy from music ; but the joys that come from constant, intimate contact with beautiful works—joys similar to those you derive from perusing your favourite books whenever the whim takes you, comparing one work or passage with another, dwelling upon any that stimulates your imagination or otherwise interests you—will be denied to you.

Of the contrivances which may serve as substitutes for reading music and playing I shall have a word to say presently. Meanwhile, let us keep to the point that theoretical knowledge alone will enable you to play or read music, and therefore to conduct your investigations according to your own plan.

This is the sole positive advantage of theoretical knowledge from the music lover's point of view. Theory will not assist you in forming your taste. Indeed, if you rest content with the homœopathic doses of theory and science provided in current books on Musical Appreciation, you may be hampered rather than aided.

In the speech he delivered on the day when the Paris *Schola Cantorum* was opened, Vincent d'Indy, its director, said :

' I have never failed to notice that the " good " public, the public which is genuinely responsive to fine music, consists of two fractions only : people who have a thorough knowledge of the art of music—these are very few—and people who know nothing, but listen earnestly and simple-heartedly. The " bad " public, which bandies words but does not know how to listen, consists of people who possess a smattering of theory. Being no longer unsophisticated enough to feel moved, because they think themselves learned, while they are not learned enough to judge soundly, they can neither understand nor enjoy.'

It is impossible to state more forcibly the reasons why semi-knowledge is bound to interfere with the listener's capacity for enjoyment and to stunt and warp his judgement. Semi-knowledge is an unavoidable stage between ignorance and the adequate, unprejudiced knowledge which so few of us may hope to achieve. But you will be safe so long as you remember that theoretical knowledge, however extensive, provides no standard for the appraisement of art.

I have told you as much before, and pointed out how theory assists you in training your ear and memory. This is the essential matter for you. Start training your ear and memory at once : listen to music as often and as carefully as you can. When you are listening carelessly, you are spoil-ing your capacity to enjoy music as much as you spoil your hand for billiards when you ' just knock the balls about ' Train your memory by listening to the same music again and again : not in order to know it by heart mechanically (some people fancy that they ' understand ' a piece when they are able to hum or strum or describe it from memory), but so as to realize its order, the bearing of its parts on one another, and to become so familiar with it that nothing of the structure and texture to which it owes its power to convey impressions of beauty will remain hidden from you.

Strive to extend the circle of your likes as soon as possible, though without undue haste. When you feel that the time has come for you to tackle music which does not appeal to you particularly, but which people whose opinions you consider trustworthy love and extol, do not be discouraged if at first you make no headway with it. Leave it aside for a time, and revert to it later. In the meanwhile you will have had other experiences by which your responsiveness and elasticity will have been increased. Every time you master the secret of one work of art, you acquire a fresh capacity for discrimination and enjoyment. You may, at the start, remain indifferent to the beauties of Bach's fugues and partitas or Beethoven's sonatas, and feel differently later, after a closer acquaintanceship with Mozart or Schumann or Franck or Borodin has whetted your appetite and sharpened your wits. Or, of course, it may be Bach or Beethoven's music that will prepare you better to enjoy the music of the others.

Do not imagine for a moment that you or anybody will ever acquire the capacity to enjoy all the best music (that is, all the music that has been found best by a great majority of music lovers) equally deeply. There is no reason of principle why this should be impossible : but in point of fact it hardly ever occurs if it occurs at all. None of us is without constitutional, sometimes ineradicable idiosyncrasies which may lead him to see works otherwise than other people will. Perhaps no two human beings see the same music in exactly the same light, although there are countless works and countless points in each of these works on whose import most educated music lovers belonging to the same civilization agree in the main.

You, as a beginner, will be well advised to proceed with

humility and diffidence, realizing that the likes and dislikes of a majority of experienced music lovers carry greater weight than your own or than of any one human being. But a time will come for you, as for every music lover, when you will be justified in feeling yourself sufficiently experienced to decide, in the last resort, according to your own intuition. You will still be ready to profit by the experience of others; but you will know that you are able to test their assertions as well as your own, and have the right to decide for yourself. This time comes far sooner for the music lover pure and simple than for the critic or teacher, upon whom the responsibility rests of guiding others. But with professional advisers and plain music lovers alike, the definiteness and clarity of outlook that come with experience are widely different from the peremptoriness of the unenlightened.

On the question of the respective advantages of a fastidious taste and a catholic taste I shall say nothing, because nothing I could say could be really useful. If you are intended by nature to be fastidious or catholic in taste, experience may alter your natural inclination : but I doubt if it will, and am certain that nothing else would. My object is to show you how to acquire experience, trusting to the consequences.

So far as ear training is concerned, singing (with an adequate backing of theoretical knowledge) and violin playing (or playing any bowed instrument) are perhaps best. Any instrument properly studied is good. The piano has one great advantage over all others, because it enables you to play, not only the music originally written for this instrument—which includes more than enough to provide a thorough education of taste and a lifetime of enjoyment—but arrangements of practically every kind of music written. Learn both to interpret works—that is, to play them correctly and intelligently—and to read at sight. Both are useful, and each serves a distinct purpose.

Do not imagine, however, that your object in learning to

play the violin or the piano is to learn to appreciate skill in
piano or violin playing. This is one of the fallacies which I
grieve to encounter in books on Appreciation and also in
other writings on music. I shall tell you in the chapter *The
Taste for The Music* why I wish you, during these first stages,
never to devote a thought to the skill displayed by inter-
preters and composers.

A story told of the French actor Dugazon (a pupil of the
famous Talma) will meanwhile make the point more clear.
He was behind the stage during an interval of *Othello*.
Suddenly—it was, we are told, in consequence of a wager—
he made his appearance in front of the curtain and started
counting : ‘ One footlight—two footlights—three footlights . . . ’ and so on, giving his voice so skilful and so
wide a variety of inflections that he held the audience spell-
bound, as under the influence of some tremendous drama,
and was finally greeted with loud applause. Similar things
often occur nowadays on the concert platform, but with this
difference, that the audience does not usually appear to
realize that it is being given just ‘ footlights ’. Do not allow
yourself to be misled by your enjoyment of skill.

Playing the piano—especially if you are able to play at
sight—you will in a large measure be independent of outside assistance, and able to become familiar with practically
all the works you choose. Remember that a considerable
proportion of the classical repertory, and even a larger proportion of contemporary music, are never played in public :
even in a great city such as London you may spend years
and years without having an opportunity to hear certain
works you wish, or are recommended, to know. Learn to
play duets if you can find a partner. It will enable you to get
acquainted with many fine works not available in transcriptions for piano solo. Even where a choice exists, transcriptions for piano duet are often more faithful.

If you wish to learn to play, do not select your teacher at
random. Many of those who offer to teach the piano or theory

in a few weeks—and perhaps without ever seeing you and hearing you play—will not only cause you to waste your time and money, but may absolutely wreck your chances of ever learning properly. Nothing could be more hopelessly stultifying than certain of the so-called simplified methods of tuition in music, languages, and many other things. Remember, moreover, that the principles of playing and reading are simple enough ; but it is practice, and only practice, that makes for their proper application.

If you do not play, the best is to keep in touch with some friend who does ; if it is possible, small meetings might be organized at which works can be read and discussed in common. The smaller and more informal the meeting the better : this will not only ensure a proper atmosphere, but render interchange of views far easier. Comments on the works played, culled from books or periodicals, might also be read and discussed.

At such meetings, try your best not to waste one another's time nor divert one another's attention. Do not be afraid of offering and inviting remarks or suggestions, nor of threshing out, now and then, some relevant point : but do not aim at becoming a debating society. When speaking of music, it is fatally easy even for experts to drift away into mere word-spinning.

For the purposes of study, if you do not play, or pending the time when you will be able to read music fluently, a piano-player will enable you to hear, in the originals or in transcriptions, most of the classics and a reasonable, if not altogether satisfactory, proportion of modern works. If, however, you develop an interest in comparatively little-known works, old or new, you will frequently be disappointed to find that they are not available. This again shows that there is nothing like learning to play for yourself.

The piano-player is the one form of mechanical assistance whose defects, although not small, are not of a kind that makes me fear lest recourse to it will exercise a nefarious

influence on the education of your taste and especially of your musical ear. I can say as much of no other. My objections to talking-machines and to the wireless is that they disfigure the quality and balance of tone of practically all music you hear through them, and therefore tend to coarsen and blunt your ear. It is a great pity that it should be thus, because for cheapness and convenience they cannot be beaten.

Mr. Francis Toye (in *The Outlook*, April 19, 1924) states the case for and against the talking-machine most accurately and reasonably thus :

' I cannot believe that the ordinary orchestral record as reproduced on the ordinary gramophone can give to the wholly uninitiated a true idea of what the orchestra really sounds like. To begin with, the volume of tone is different and the balance of the bass instruments always seems to me deficient. I am the last person in the world to underrate the utility of the gramophone ; as an adjunct, as an aid to memory, as a useful makeshift, it performs invaluable service: but facts are facts, and no one was ever the worse for facing them.

' All that a child will know is that the Beethoven Symphony it hears at school does not sound so well as "Kitten on the Keys," which it listens to at home—with the result that it may, not unnaturally, find more pleasure in the latter. I do myself.

' The fact of the matter is that music remains, primarily, the art of beautiful sound and attractive rhythms. This is often lost sight of in a fog of emotional, intellectual, and even moral considerations, but nothing can quite take the place of the physical sensation caused by the sound or the rhythm on the brain. It is this that causes the delicious shiver, the quickened pulse which are the essence of musical enjoyment. It is to this, the highest, the most acute pleasure known to many of us, that we would wish to introduce the young in early life, so that, in later years, they may be able to realize the loveliness of the art.'

Another couple of quotations will show that this view is not merely that of one or two extremists. In *Musical Opinion* (November 1923), ' Schaunard ' wrote :

' The only term befitting is nastiness. A musical performance may be as greatly improved by the wireless receiver as it is at present rather worsened. One thing alone is almost certain : it will never be made to sound exactly the same when heard through receiving instruments as it does to the listener within the room. The gramophone is a similar case.'

In the *Monthly Musical Record* (April 1924) Mr. Richard Capell writes of Elgar's E flat symphony as heard by him on the wireless :

' What was made of it by those who did not already know the work I cannot think.'

And in the *Sunday Times* (March 15, 1924) Mr. Ernest Newman wrote :

' I gave a number of instances in which the wireless quite altered the scoring of the *Tannhäuser* Overture, and my list could have been extended greatly. If what I heard on that and other occasions is the best that wireless can do, then I can only say that what the listener-in hears of a big orchestral work is the merest travesty of the original. Captain Eckersley is quite correct in saying that it is near enough to give the average listener a fair idea of the work ; if a man just wants to be sure of the tunes, does not mind the harmonies being often perverted, and is quite satisfied with orchestral timbres of which the composer never dreamed, then wireless is good enough for him, and none of us will grudge him the pleasure he gets out of it. But I repeat that, for the critical musician, the transmission is a travesty of the original. It may be better that two million people, many of whom would be otherwise shut out from music, should get a great work in an imperfect form than not get it at all. But nothing is to be gained by our denying the obvious imperfections of the present wireless transmission of music on the large scale.'

Therefore, when resorting to the wireless and talking-machine you should at least know that you are not always giving a fair chance either to the music or to yourself. I am writing this in the year 1924, with the knowledge that manufacturers, as a rule, are not unaware of these shortcomings, and are striving to remedy them. All of us earnestly hope that they may succeed.

For the purpose of memory-training, the talking-machine is useful to those who do not play. But whether you use it or not, always make the utmost of circumstances. Miss no chance of hearing music played. Attend concerts as often as possible. Again, never try to combine analysing works and listening to them for enjoyment. If you are fortunate enough to attend many concerts, you may decide that certain portions of the time may better be devoted to study than to enjoyment, with a view to training your ear and memory. You will greatly benefit by the sacrifices thus made during the first stages of your experiences as a music-lover in order to hasten the acquisition of the power to discriminate.

As a general rule, select for this purpose of study a few works of sterling, tested merit, such as string quartets and symphonies by Haydn, Mozart, and Beethoven. You need not fear that the temporary drudgery of studying these piecemeal will mar your enjoyment of them on other occasions. It is only when aiming at a combination or a compromise that you—and also your advisers—run the risk of achieving neither adequate study nor genuine enjoyment.

CHAPTER V

WHAT MUSIC IS

T H I S chapter and the following are written in view of the time when you will feel the need to study theory—a time which I think is bound to come for two out of every three of you. Meanwhile, you may skip them if you wish, after having noted that they bear upon two points : the fact that music consists of sounds grouped together so as to be inter-related and constitute a whole ; and the fact—it *is* a fact for all unprejudiced observers of musical facts—that any principles according to which they are grouped and interrelated are rather a matter of choice and habit than of natural necessity and unavoidable law. Hence the advisability of listening to music as music only—this is explained in the chapter *The Taste for the Music*—and the need to listen with an open mind, never believing that good music must conform to this or that particular rule laid down in books on theory or even in books on Appreciation. Now you may skip straight on to page 46.

On the other hand, if you insist on reading these chapters, please consider them as intended to give you a mere plan for a course which should be carried out with the help of other books on theory. I am only trying to show you in which light you, the music lover, are to understand the information provided by these books, and what the principles of theory finally boil down to. You will realize that my survey is very rough and ready, and simplified to the utmost. In other words, my object is to provide you with a compass and not a chart.

The most general way, and the best, of defining music is to say that it consists of sounds grouped according to certain orders of relation.

The human mind has found no better way of defining the work of art, be it poem or prose, symphony or picture or cathedral, than to say that it constitutes a definite, intelligible, and independent whole whose parts are in close relation and co-operation, so that when you confront it you find it fully satisfactory in itself, for what it is, without feeling the need for anything outside it or beside it to render it satisfactory.

Let us put this in plainer language. A good picture or statue satisfies you without your having to ask yourself what or whom it represents, or which circumstances dictated the attitude it shows. It tells you all you need know in order to find it beautiful and satisfying as a picture or a statue ; the same occurs with a good piece of writing. The circumstances that prompted Shakespeare to write his sonnets have nothing to do with the value of those sonnets as sonnets.

Of all arts it is music that embodies best this ideal definition of art. It consists of sounds forming patterns, related and contrasted so as to make a whole which is entirely self-contained and independent, and as such must either satisfy us or leave us unsatisfied. Theory can only deal with the various ways in which sounds are combined, without ever helping us to know why certain combinations are profoundly moving, certain wholes profoundly satisfactory, and other very nearly similar combinations and wholes leave us unmoved.

Let us forget for a while the existence or even the possibility of rules, and ask ourselves what a composer, intent on writing a piece of music, would do in order to ensure that this piece be an intelligible and satisfactory whole.

In the first place he would select, out of the infinite variety of available sounds, a limited number of sounds. Then he would arrange these into patterns and these patterns into a whole, exactly as the writer arranges words and the painter lines and colours, but with this all-important difference that sounds cannot stand as symbols or representations of

ideas or objects in the same way as words and lines and colours do. Thus he is compelled to find the principle of the arrangement mainly within himself or in a certain convention, not in the facts of the outer world. It is easy to see that convention alone does not provide a satisfactory principle. Every artistic convention originates in something that was first done instinctively, and ceases to serve its purpose when it is followed mechanically.

Composers found within themselves quite a number of things to get on with : they felt that certain combinations were exhilarating, others depressing ; that some suggested movement and others repose, and some continued and magnified the inflexions of speech and cry of satisfaction, surprise, anxiety, pain, and so forth. They were endowed, like all human beings, with a sense of the value of order, analogy, and contrast ; with imagination ; and also with a capacity for acquiring habits.

All these idiosyncrasies and ways of feeling play their part in our appreciation of music as well as in musical composition. And it is chiefly habits that are responsible for the excessive importance ascribed to the alleged fixed natural laws of musical composition and appreciation.

It stands to reason that a law or convention of some kind is necessary. Otherwise music would no more exist than languages or games would. Tennis, for instance, would not be possible without a rule to the effect that the ball must fall into a certain part of the court, and must not be caught with the hand or kicked back. If it is found that the waiving of an old rule or the introduction of a new rule will improve the game, the rules will be altered, and nobody will dream of insisting upon judging the new game by the old laws : for the object is the game, and the laws are only means. It is by a process of this kind that whist gave birth to bridge and bridge to auction bridge. You may say that whist is a better game than bridge : but you will never play bridge well nor enjoy it properly if the old whist habits cling to you.

I shall have more to say about habits in a further chapter: meanwhile, let me point out that there is very little in musical laws and habits that rests on a scientifically determinable basis. Even for so common a thing as the minor scale of our music, no unquestionable scientific explanation has ever been found; and the variety of explanations suggested is most instructive in a way. The best explanation ever given is altogether unscientific, although quite relevant from the artistic point of view. It is that the minor scale, being the most thoroughly contrasted with the major, was retained together with it for reasons of aesthetic choice. How far the retention of the major mode was also a matter of aesthetic choice will presently be shown.

The ancient Greeks, the Chinese, the Hindoos, the Arabs, to whom music meant or means as much as to any of us, and whose other arts rest on principles either quite similar to or as easily acceptable to us as our own, had, or still have, entirely different systems of musical rules and habits. Until we get rid of some of our habits, we find it difficult to appreciate Chinese music ; and the Chinese find it difficult to appreciate European music until they get rid of some of their habits. A curious instance of the length to which people sometimes go when they erect their habits into a system is afforded by the statement which a German writer made that ' it is through losing its sensitiveness to minute differences of pitch that the ear becomes capable of enjoying exotic music'. This, in fact, is the very reverse of the truth. It really means that by overlooking minute differences in pitch, you may succeed in considering the scales used in exotic music as similar to the usual European scales—that is, enjoy them not for what they are but for what they are not, simply because our habits or conventions stand in the way of our enjoying them for what they are (if we are to enjoy them at all).

But of course it was needful to select a limited number of definite tones or notes out of the infinite number of possible tones, exactly as in order to have an alphabet we must adopt a limited number of definite letters. And for the same reason, a limited number of definite relationships between tones were selected and organized into a system, exactly as letters are organized into words, and words into a language.

A few elementary facts of nature, such as the compass of the singing voice and certain unavoidable conditions of instrument building, played a part in the choice. But the main point always remained that composers should avoid scattering their efforts on a greater number and variety of resources that they could acquire ready command of, and than their listeners could readily absorb. ' Too many notes ' is a common complaint of people whose habits are rudely battered by new departures in music. It has been uttered against Monteverde's music and Mozart's, Beethoven's and Wagner's—to name only these few.

An all-important factor in the choice of notes to get on with was the physical fact that if you blow through a pipe or pluck a string and get a certain definite tone, other tones occur as by-products (this will be referred to in the following chapter). The first of these is always what is called the octave, that is, a sound higher in pitch but otherwise identical with the original sound. The identity of octaves is as clear to the listener as it is to the theorist. In point of fact, if a man starts singing a tune and a woman, whose voice is naturally higher in pitch, joins in, she will instinctively and unavoidably sing in the higher octave. Hence, for musical art, an element of limitation and symmetry which was readily adopted, and is useful and elastic enough to have become permanent as well as universal.

Within the compass of the octave, a limited number of tones form the scale. Some are directly selected from the number of the by-products which I have mentioned (whose technical name is overtones or partial tones). Others have a less simple origin. This, however, need not detain us just now. Our point is that familiarity with a scale—

whatever the constitution of this scale—plays a great part
in our perception of relationships between its constituent
notes : exactly the part that familiarity with words plays in
our understanding of a language, in fact. Non-familiarity
may lead us to explain a scale as being ' out of tune '—which
is just how our German author disposes of exotic scales.

The need to dwell upon such points would not exist
but for the misapprehensions that are continuously being
fostered. One writer coolly states that ' music is expression
according to rule', which is true in a way, but would be
truer if he continued by telling his readers that the number
of possible and acceptable rules is infinite. Another advises
us to find out ' how far a work conforms with or departs
from the accepted rules of harmony and counterpoint '.

This particular author rightly points out that ' nothing
but chaotic confusion could result where anything may be
right and nothing may be wrong'. But to say as much is only
to have a tilt at windmills. No true artist—nor even, it might
be added, any impostor—has ever conceived a course of
procedure in which everything may be right and nothing
wrong. The futurist school, for instance, includes people
who, far from telling you that nothing may be wrong, say
that everything done so far is hopelessly wrong. And the
genuine artist, even when he innovates most daringly, works
according to a certain scheme and invites you to accept or
reject the scheme on the strength of the results, never the
results on the strength of the scheme.

This means that he obeys a law of some sort, which may
be partly or almost wholly new—new at least to us, his
hearers. What the practical consequences for us may be is
explained further (pp. 44 and 71). Meanwhile, let me just
point out that nothing I have said or shall say aims at dis-
paraging the laws which are illustrated in the works of the
great composers of past periods, nor at dissuading you from
studying them as thoroughly as you may care to do. These
laws, indeed, are just so many means which they adopted

in order to secure unity, proportion, and logic. To realize what these means are will therefore not prove useless to you. But my real object is to show you, and to make you actually feel, that musical beauty or ugliness cannot be explained as easily as it may be felt ; and that, exactly as a musical work is never beautiful just because it conforms to a certain set of rules, so it is never ugly just because it does not. If you realize this much, it will save you no end of trouble—at times with your own self because it will warn you against your own prejudices or habits, at times with what other people say or write about music, because it will put you on guard against their possible prejudices or short-sightedness.

CHAPTER VI

MATERIALS, RULES, AND FACTS OF MUSIC

T H E R E are four ways in which sounds may differ from one another, and four only :

Duration—i.e. relative length and shortness.

Intensity—i.e. relative loudness (or stress) and softness (non-stress).

Pitch—i.e. relative height.

Colour or quality—depending on conditions of production (instruments or voices).

This short list covers all the raw materials of music.

The principles governing the relationships between sounds range from identity or contrast pure and simple to the subtlest shades of affinity or variation, analogy or difference. Notes combined with one another, in succession and simultaneously, form patterns each of which, roughly speaking, is a unit. And these units in turn form greater units between which relationships of similar kinds exist, and so on until the piece, or whole, is complete.

The first property of a pattern is rhythm. As soon as notes follow one another, a relationship between their respective duration or intensity is established, and rhythm begins to exist. Whenever identical sounds of identical duration follow one another in regular succession—such as the ticking of a clock—we instinctively divide them into small groups (generally of two or three, these being the simplest divisions). This means that we conceive them as interrelated, we create the rudiment of a rhythmical structure. This we cannot do except by imagining a difference between these identical sounds ; and this difference will be one of intensity. That is, we imagine one sound in every two or three

to be marked by a certain emphasis called stress or accent. We generally consider that the stress marks the beginning of each group, because it is our landmark and therefore a convenient starting point. Failing some kind if periodicity, we could no more reduce sounds to any kind of order than we could count without arranging our numbers into tens and hundreds or dozens and grosses or whatever it may be.

In actual music, of course, we are not left to imagine a relationship between stress and non-stress. If identical notes follow one another, the performer is shown where to mark the stress. Nor are stresses—that is, accents—necessarily the beginning of a group or period. They may be starting points, centres, or goals. They may occur at regular intervals or at irregular. There may be principal accents and secondary accents.

Of course, the relationships that are easiest of all to create and to perceive are founded on a regular order of recurrence. From this elementary fact to the fixed idea that a melody, or any kind of musical phrase, must consist of units arranged in symmetrical periods is not a far step. The practice of writing melodies that conform to this definition is certainly frequent among composers of all times and countries. Theory, therefore, cannot ignore it. But theorists go wrong when they lay down the law that no other course is admissible, and try to show (as is actually done in a certain German book on Bach's music) that when a great master has written a phrase consisting of seven bars or of ten, it should be really understood as consisting of the regulation eight bars with one left out, or two added.

Composers of instrumental music began by giving greater prominence to the simpler orders of rhythmical periodicity, with which they were best capable of dealing, and which their listeners could more easily perceive. Then with experience came the capacity to handle and to perceive more complex elements. The rhythmical structure of a symphony by Beethoven is far more elaborate than that of a symphony by Haydn, which in turn contains a far greater variety of rhythmical combinations than any instrumental work of the seventeenth century.

As soon as contrasts of pitch as well as of intensity or duration intervene, we have melody—a much discussed thing and a much misused word. What constitutes melody in the current sense of the term is a point on which people will go on disagreeing for ever. It has been said of almost every great master in his time that his music lacked melody. The reason for utterances of this kind is very well explained by Mr. Edwin Evans in his little book, *The Margin of Music* (Oxford University Press), as follows :

' I have long felt convinced that the only tenable definition of melody is : a succession of single notes so arranged that their mutual relations are those to which the ear is accustomed—in short, that melody is chiefly our recognition of the familiar. The ear grows inured to certain inflections, sequences of notes, and *bouts de phrases* ; and when these are present in sufficient number to create a suggestion of old friendship, but at the same time their arrangement conveys a feeling of freshness, the result to the average man is melody.'

However, I am using the word here in its general sense and not in its more restricted usual sense.

It is with regard to the selection of a limited and co-ordinated range of notes that natural facts afforded the greatest help to musicians. At the start, as I have stated, is the fact that a vibrating body (column of air in a pipe, or string) gives a note of a certain pitch and accessorily a certain number of higher notes, called overtones or partial tones.

Here is a note with its first few partial tones :

The note numbered 2, the first overtone, is the octave of the original note. It is always produced by a speed of vibration exactly twice that which produces the original note. So, if you double the speed again you have a fresh octave, the note marked 4 in the figure. A speed of vibration three times that which produces the original note produces the note marked 3, whose natural relation to the original note is therefore the simplest conceivable outside that of the octave —which we have roughly defined as one of identity in a higher region of sound. Double the speed that produces 3 and you have 6, which repeats 3 an octave higher. After 3, the first new related sound to occur is 5, produced by a speed five times as great as that which produced the original note. When you feel that the time has come for you to know more about these scientific facts (which are very interesting even though they are of no greater practical use to the music lover than optics to the lover of painting), you can do no better than read Dr. Buck's *Scope of Music* and *Acoustics for Musicians* (Oxford University Press). My description is very much like the rough figures that one chalks on a blackboard for the mere purpose of demonstration.

Now, if music were to follow slavishly the course indicated by the natural phenomena I have just referred to, the scale used by music would have been formed in direct accordance with this natural and very simple system of relations. But in point of fact no portion of the series of overtones of any one note will ever give you an actual major scale such as is used in classical music.

The series, it is true, gives us first of all the major triad or common chord of music, which we find in its usual form, called root-form, at 4, 5, 6 thus :

But in order to obtain all the notes of the major scale, we must seek further afield—and even then the result is not altogether satisfactory. In our example, the original note (called ground note, or tonic) being C, we need, besides the E and the G which the first overtones supply, four notes, viz. D, F, A, and B, in order to have the full sequence constituting the major diatonic scale whose ground note or tonic is C—that is

Three of these four we find much higher up in the series of overtones : D is 9, B is 15, and A is 27. Intervening overtones such as 7, 11, 13, and others are not admitted in the primary form of the scale (most of them are used in practice under the name of chromatically altered notes) ; and there remains the note, F, which we cannot find although we find near approximations to it at 21 and at 43.

In other words, the usual major diatonic scale of music, which so many theorists have represented as the direct product of an unavoidable law of nature, consists of notes whose natural relationships are not the simplest possible, but comparatively complex. These relationships can be expressed in figures thus if we avail ourselves of the facility afforded by the identity of octaves (16 = 8 x 2, 20 = 5 x 4, etc.) : 16, 18, 20, 21 (approximately), 24, 27, 30.

If, instead of following the series of overtones, we seek in an altogether different direction, we find a far simpler principle to account for the relationships existing between the notes of our scale.

Let us suppose that besides the pipe or string giving the ground note C we have another one giving the ground note G (that is the note whose relation to C is the simplest conceivable apart from identity), the first few overtones of G will give us the triad

whose relation with C is obvious, and which provides two
of the needful notes. If we also have a pipe or string giving
a ground note that will stand in relation to C exactly as C
stands in relation to G (again, the simplest relation outside
identity, expressed by the figures 2 :: 3), this ground note
itself will be another of the needed notes, namely F, which
stands a fifth below C (or a fourth above) exactly as C stands
a fifth below G (or a fourth above), and the first partials
will include the last needed note, A :

Let us now consider our three chords together, with the
closeness and simplicity of the relationship between them—
notice that each of them has one note in common with the
central or tonic triad :

Then, by a further application of the principle of the
identity of octaves, let us write down all the notes one after
the other in their closest possible order. This gives us the
scale of C major :

which only roughly resembles the scale that we find between
overtones 8 and 16 of our first example, and is characterized
by the fact that it consists of whole-tones and semitones in
a certain order. From the tonic to the octave, it can be divided
into two exactly symmetrical halves. It is both highly organized and plastic, and provides, therefore, splendid material

to work on : but its coming into being was determined by
aesthetic choice and not under the influence of natural laws
only. The interval of the semitone is the smallest admitted
in the musical system which I am now describing. The
whole-tone intervals which occur between notes of the C
major diatonic scale are divided into two semitones, where-
by the chromatic scale comes into being. A proportion of
readers will probably be aware that just now attempts are
being made to utilize, beside semitones, quarter-tones ;
and that intervals smaller than the semitone were used in
Greek music and elsewhere.

Any note in the scale can, of course, be the starting-point,
or tonic, of a scale ; so that we have, as shall presently be
explained, as many scales as there are notes ; and each scale
is related to any other exactly in the same fashion as notes
of one scale are related to one another. This principle, jointly
with the principle of rhythmic relationship, is the foundation
of current rules of form.

The relationship between any two notes of a scale depends
primarily upon their relation to the centre or tonic. The note
C, for instance, plays the main part in the key of C major,
since it is the very centre, but a very secondary part in the
key of B flat major. The relationship between C and G is
the very keystone of tonality in C major, but no longer so in
B flat major.

Again I remind you that I am not attempting a full
description of the materials of music. Books on theory will
provide all the needful information about the terms I use,
about scales and keys, major and minor, and all other points
which I barely touch or omit altogether.

Accessorily, the relationship between any two notes
depends upon their proximity. The relationship between
C and D, or D and E flat, etc., is always obvious, whatever
the key and apart from any notion of key, so long as they
are close to one another for the ear, and for the eye when
written down. But if the distance is increased, the relation-

ship is less easily felt by the ear. A passage such as the following :

sounds altogether flowing and clear. But a modern composer may achieve an effect of strangeness simply by widening its intervals thus ·

Once a scheme such as that of tonality is adopted, it is essential that the part played by the tonic, with its triad as centre, and by the other two determining notes (in C major, G and F, called respectively dominant and sub-dominant) with their triads, should be unequivocal. This was most easily achieved by giving these notes and chords prominence, by using them more frequently than others and especially at crucial points, such as the beginning and end of phrases, accented beats, and so forth. This practice soon gave birth to rules devised so as to ensure that the practice should be followed, and to restrict or forbid all causes of ambiguity.

In proportion as composers acquired a subtler insight into the possibilities of relationships between notes and chords, they extended the range of their practice. This they did far more quickly than theory could follow. Consequently, whenever a composer of genius cropped up, some theorist or other was almost sure to be found averring that his innovations were no good, because they broke the rules. Later on, of course, rules were established to cover innovations which had proved fruitful.

I cannot demonstrate here the principle behind each particular rule of theory. But a few examples may show that every rule aims at ensuring clear and definite relationships between notes used in music. This is obvious as regards the rule already referred to, that tonic, dominant, and sub-dominant, should be given due prominence in a triad scheme, or the rule prohibiting leaps such as shown in the last musical example above. But leaps from one note of a chord to any other note of the same chord are not prohibited because the harmonic relationship remains clear although contiguity no longer helps the ear. Another rule forbids two consecutive leaps in the same direction, also because this would go against the principle of contiguity. The rule that prescribed the preparation and resolution of discords was intended to ensure that a note used simultaneously with other notes, even if it is distantly related to these other notes, should be closely related to other notes in the nearest propinquity, and understood by all to be related. Thus in a combination such as

in which D is, comparatively speaking, distantly related to the chord C E G, the offending note D had to be introduced first by a chord to which it actually belonged and to resolve itself by descending to C:

Another rule allows certain otherwise prohibited melodic leaps and relations if they occur in the course of what is called a sequence—that is, an ascending or descending repetition of a combination just heard before. This shows that the object of the rule is to ensure that whatever happens in music should be unambiguously referable to the main scheme in which it occurs, and understood as a matter of course.

All this, in principle, was excellent, but—as the further evolution of music has shown—should not be taken literally for purposes of appreciation, any more than the rules of form, which are applications on a larger scale of the very same principles.

It was pointed out on p. 40 that there are as many scales or keys as there are semitones in the scale. Your theoretical books will tell you all about the fact called enharmony and the practice called temperament rendered possible by this fact, which has rendered it possible to restrict the number of notes and keys used—which in fact could be infinite. In practice, exactly as there are seven notes to the diatonic scale, so we have seven successive keys in the ascending order from C, the second being G, the third D, and so on by fifths upwards ; and seven from C downwards, the first being F, the second B flat, and so on by fifths. This gives us fifteen major keys, because D flat is admitted besides C sharp, G flat besides F sharp, and C flat besides B ; and fifteen minor keys. There is also the possibility of branching into further extensions, such as G sharp major, dominant of C sharp, and so on. But, as you will see when studying questions of enharmony, the circle is closed by the fact that G sharp is the equivalent of A flat. Some convention of this kind was needed in order to limit the number of keys, exactly as one was needed to limit the number of notes in the scale.

A melody, a period, and even a whole piece of music may be in one key throughout, or pass from one key to another. But no big structural scheme such as that of the fugue or the sonata was possible without modulation or change of key. In such structures the order and balance of

keys was made (and in the wake of practice came a rule
to the effect that it should be) similar to the order and balance
of notes and chords within the compass of one key.

In proportion as experience grew, composers discovered
that the principle of unity in variety which had dictated first
the practice and afterwards the rules was far more elastic
than the rules made it out to be. Beethoven, for instance,
gave a great shock to theorists by beginning his first symphony not with an unequivocal proclamation of its key as
was considered right, proper, and unavoidable, but with a
chord out of the key. Later, composers started dispensing
with the traditional tonal formula or cadence for ending
phrases, sections, and pieces. They even dispensed with a
return to the initial key at the end of pieces. Nowadays a
good many of them write music in which nothing can be
found to conform to the theoretical notion of key, while
others have resorted to the hitherto unexampled procedure
of using several keys simultaneously.

All this may be baffling and unwelcome to people who
believe that the conditions of musical art are determined
by natural laws. This is why I have written this chapter in
order to show you that they were determined largely by
aesthetic choice, and that the same order of considerations
which determined them may lead to their being extended
again and again. One fine day you may find yourself listening with delight to Balakiref's *Tamara*, and thenceforth you
will feel no patience with writers who tell you that it is badly
constructed because it does not end in the initial key ; or
to some lovely example of what is called ' atonal ' music,
and you will vow never again to allow yourself to be bothered
with technical rules or considerations. Or, if you docilely
admit that rule-mongers are right and you yourself wrong,
you will forfeit something of your own capacity to discriminate instead of increasing it. Both results are equally undesirable. The fact that a principle may be wrongly understood or applied does not mean that the principle itself is

valueless. But in any case, you must understand a principle thoroughly before you are able to decide whether it is rightly or wrongly applied or overlooked.

As a music lover eager to extend the quality and range of your musical enjoyment, you should study theory diligently for the additional insight it gives you into the works of composers on whose practice theory is based, and for the experience which the study enables you to acquire. If, following my advice, you seek assistance in books that are purely devoted to theory and not to linking theory and appreciation together, you will run less risk of being led astray.

There can be no question that knowledge is useful. If you were asked whether, all other things such as keenness, sensitiveness, and imagination being equal, a good English scholar does not enjoy more things in Shakespeare than an indifferent English scholar, you would consider the reply obvious.

But, as the French philosopher, Bergson, has put it: 'the writer's art ultimately lies in his making us forget that he uses words'. So does the composer's art ultimately lie in making us forget that he uses notes. Theory, which is constantly reminding you of notes and the arrangement of notes, is the last thing in the world of which you should think when you set out to appraise a composer's art. This is equally true whether the work you are attempting to appraise be one about which current theory can tell you quite a lot—for instance, a Bach fugue—or one about which theory can tell you hardly anything except that it does not conform to rules.

CHAPTER VII

TASTE AND TASTES

I T is wofully easy to blunder when talking of taste. The word itself is not difficult to define : but it has at least three distinct meanings. It may mean a leaning towards a certain thing : you have a taste for music or you have not. It may mean a tendency to prefer certain things to certain others : to like vocal music better than instrumental music, or the violin better than the piano, or Chopin's music better than Debussy's, or Debussy's *Prélude à l'Après Midi d'un Faune* better than his *Nocturnes*.

But the third meaning holds out a danger-signal, because it stands for the capacity of telling good from bad in an apparently absolute, not relative, way. The man who derives more enjoyment from the latest music-hall tune or drawing-room piece than from a Mozart quartet or a Beethoven symphony is sure that his taste is as good as the next man's if not better ; anyhow, he feels that it is good enough for him. A composer of ballads was asking, quite recently, ' why millions of people should be deprived of the songs they like simply because of a few highbrows '.

This danger-signal should not be made into a bogy. Taste is essentially the power to enjoy coupled with the power to discriminate. And as soon as you begin to discriminate you begin to make distinctions between better and less good. You are out for enjoyment. So are, with a very few easily discoverable exceptions, the alleged ' highbrows '. They are really what Bennett calls 'the passionate few '. Again I copy from his *Literary Taste*, using the word ' music ' where he uses the word ' literature ' :

' They find a keen and lasting pleasure in music. The recurrence of this pleasure naturally keeps their interest in

music very much alive. They are forever making new re-
searches, forever practising on themselves. They learn to
understand themselves and to know what they want. They
do not enjoy to-day what will seem tedious to-morrow.
When they find a work tedious, no amount of popular chatter
will persuade them that it is pleasurable ; and when they
find it pleasurable no chill silence of the street crowds will
affect their conviction that the work is good and permanent.'

They are simply inviting you to share joys which they
know by experience to be the most desirable. Their attitude
and yours, in the long run, point to the same selfish object.
' Which would you rather, sing a hymn tune or be given a
doughnut ? ' may be a difficult problem ; but it ceased to
be one to the little boy who knew that if he chose the hymn
tune he would get two doughnuts instead of one. Well, the
passionate few are showing you the way to getting that
second doughnut. You are able to benefit by their experience.

Your object in educating your taste is to do away with
everything that might render your enjoyment of music less
speedy, less frequent, less certain, less keen, and less lasting.
The doughnut is certainly worth getting, even if it means
that you will have to develop certain idiosyncrasies of yours
and try to check certain others, and perhaps to acquire
idiosyncrasies that strike you as weird and fruitless. Indeed,
it may seem that the prospect is too good to be true : yet it
includes nothing that the true, experienced music lover does
not expect as a matter of course and get unfailingly. His
enjoyment of music is constantly growing keener and ex-
tending in scope, because every single work that he learns
to enjoy lastingly gives him a thousandfold more enjoyment
than he could get from all the music that experience teaches
him to discard if his instinct has not taught him to.

The two current sayings, ' no accounting for tastes ' and
' no disputing about tastes ' have done, and are still doing,
a lot of harm. Let us, in the light of what I have just pointed
out, try to find out how far they are true.

I shall have, I think, no difficulty in showing you that in art practically all likes and dislikes can be accounted for; and that, after this is done, it becomes easy to see how far you can profitably dispute about any particular kind of taste.

If you decided not to skip the previous two chapters, you will have realized that music consists of sounds, of a comparatively small number of sounds selected from the infinite variety of possible sounds, and differing in pitch, intensity, duration, and quality or colour. These sounds are combined into patterns, melodic, harmonic, and polyphonic (except for the purposes of ear training and theoretical study, you need never, in the whole course of the education of your taste, give a thought to these distinctions), and organized into phrases and periods which in turn are organized into a whole which is a piece of music.

If you have skipped the two chapters, the above summary of their contents, however rough and ready, will serve my present purpose. All that I wish you to bear in mind is that music consists solely of sounds organized into a whole, and that it is solely the quality and mutual relations of these sounds that constitute the materials upon which musical taste exercises itself.

There is, however, a warning which I must repeat here. It is often said that there are a natural, unquestionably right and a natural, unquestionably wrong way of regulating the organization of sounds into a whole; and that therefore to describe as nonsense certain types of modern music which seem to be composed in defiance of the natural laws to which the great classics obeyed is no matter of taste. This way of putting things does not take into account the fact that a good many of the great classics were in their time described by theorists as flying in the face of all natural laws of music.

Now to our real business. When considering the taste that prefers vocal music to instrumental, or solo singing to choral singing, or the violin to the piano, we may refer it to certain obvious, natural, almost entirely physical predispositions. But even this elementary kind of preference admits of degrees and may be influenced by education.

This suggestion will become clearer if we consider a slightly different instance. You may think somebody's voice, or tone on the violin, most delightful of all until you hear somebody else whose voice or tone strikes you as even more delightful. The more numerous your experiences of singing and violin-playing, the more definite and firm your standards of judging voices and tone will become.

Hence a first way of accounting for tastes, by adducing comparative ignorance or experience. And although judgements on such points may, in theory, be matters of pure taste, you find that in practice there is, even among moderately experienced music lovers, an almost unanimous agreement that the voice of certain singers and the tone of certain instrumentalists are supremely enjoyable. This affords a good enough foundation for ' disputing about tastes '.

Experience will likewise show you that whereas both a solo voice and a choir, or a violin and a piano, can give you enjoyment, each can do certain things which the other cannot, and therefore provide for enjoyment by different methods ; and that it is better to be able to enjoy the one as well as the other.

All remarks about voice and tone apply equally to style in singing and playing. But the matter is no longer one of physical predisposition. The quality of voice and tone appeals to your senses, but singing and playing include elements that appeal to your sensitiveness, intellect, and imagination. You may think a singer's voice magnificent, and yet fail to enjoy the use it is put to—as when you hear a simple, straightforward song sung with a wealth of elaborate melodramatic or sentimental effect or vocal ' showing-off '. Very little experience teaches one to discriminate in the same way as regards the playing of instrumental music.

E

This will be something to build upon in more ways than one. First and foremost, you may hail it as the first sign of that sense of fitness which in matters of æsthetic judgement is the last court of appeal. But no one has succeeded yet in explaining satisfactorily the foundations and working of this sense. The crude instance I give is clear enough, but I am compelled to leave the point at that. In all less crude instances the proof of the pudding is in the eating.

But you are now well on the way to acquiring a useful sense of fitness, and also to further discoveries. Without jeopardising your capacity to enjoy a lovely voice or tone (is this enjoyment not worth the sacrifice of the capacity to enjoy any kind of voice or tone indiscriminately?) you have become able to discriminate between the enjoyment which these give you and the additional enjoyment given by fine and appropriate style in interpretation. I hope and trust that sooner or later—and as soon as possible—you will give precedence to style : because although beauty of tone is an essential element, it affects but the surface of musical art, whereas interpretation reaches the very core.

This is why people find it so difficult to agree on the respective merits of interpretations. Agreement on this matter is reached only by dint of considerations almost as numerous and subtle as agreement on the quality of a piece of music.

But, sticking to my present point, let me illustrate it further. Tone is the raw material of music, exactly as clay, stone, wood, and metal are the raw materials of sculpture. You may prefer a statue made of gold to a statue made of clay ; but the preference will be artistic only so far as you are conscious that the colour, smoothess, and lustre of gold contribute to the beauty of the statue better than the colour, roughness, and dullness of clay. In other words, the merit of the statue, from the point of view of the art lover, is not commensurate with the value of the material. From his point of view, of course, it is desirable to be capable of enjoy-

ing both statues of gold and statues of clay. And when he reaches the point when he acknowledges that gold may serve an artistic purpose where clay may not, and conversely, his sense of fitness has made fresh progress.

But I am now trying to show you something even more definite. After having realized that a fine voice or tone is more enjoyable when serving the true purposes of artistic interpretation than when displayed for its own sake alone, you will begin to feel that, exactly as you are looking to the interpretations beyond the voice, you are looking to the music beyond the interpretation. Supposing that you listen to a gifted artist interpreting with equal skill a variety of musical works, you will realize that certain of these works move you more deeply or interest you more than others. Many experiences of this kind will enable you to reach a stage where even the utmost skill in interpretation, coupled with the loveliest voice or tone, will mean little to you unless you find the music interpreted worthy of attention in itself. And then, as before, when you first learnt how great the joys that a fine voice or tone can give, you will feel that you are the gainer and would far rather have the fewer and greater joys than the capacity to enjoy indiscriminately. It is a difficult, and apparently doubtful, question : but at each stage the evidence is unmistakable.

For instance, you have learnt that a fine voice or tone gives you great and certain joy, but not necessarily lasting joy. You may enjoy it two minutes, or two hours on end ; but if it is not coupled with skill in interpretation, you will eventually experience weariness and even disgust. Hence, although to enjoy a pure voice or tone is excellent taste, the taste which sets no store (be it but unconsciously) by skill in interpretation is poor.

You may think that I am exaggerating. You feel that you could listen to A——'s singing or to B——'s playing for ever, simply because of the beauty of their voice or tone. Now I need not state at length what may constitute good interpretation and what does not ; let me simply point out that if your favourites sung or played every work on their programmes in the same lovely but uninflected way, you would very soon feel bored to extinction. This shows that you *do* pay attention to points of interpretation, or at least are affected by them.

Now suppose that you are listening to the best possible interpreter and enjoying his skill thoroughly. If he goes on playing music that does not appeal to you, a time is bound to come when you will think ' I wish he would play something I *like* '. You may be listening to Miss d'Aranyi playing a Bach suite and wish she would play that jolly thing you heard the other night at the Palliseum, or to some other gifted violinist who makes you wish he would not waste his gifts on rubbish. In any case, you can, in the long run, be affected by the quality of the music played. And this fact should lead you to realize that even the most magnificent interpretation, the kind of interpretation best suited to help you to discover in a work elements of attractiveness that you never suspected, can lend but a very fleeting interest to music that is not interesting in itself. So nothing remains for you but to seek in the music itself the elements which will make for joys that are sure and keen and lasting. Then your position as a music lover will be impregnable. It is true that bad interpretations of the music you love will jar upon your feelings quite intolerably. But any reasonably good interpretation of music that appeals to you—that is any interpretation that does not distort this music, the interpretation which it is our right to expect from anybody who comes forth to play or sing—will procure you keen and lasting joy. Even your own interpretations at the piano, poor as they may be, will be enjoyable so far as they bring you into closer and more frequent contact with enjoyable music—exactly as you may enjoy reading poetry which you would be utterly incapable of reading aloud so as to cause pleasure to others. Hence the taste that places music foremost is the best taste.

When you begin to notice that different musical works affect you differently, strive to discover where the differences lie. Take an active, searching interest in the music you hear and its effects upon you. Begin by studying the effects—for it is the only thing you can do with profit just now, and the only thing that all of us do even when we appear to start at the other end (I shall qualify this statement in the next chapter).

You will easily realize that the music which attracts you arouses emotions and feelings, makes you feel elated, thrilled, or awed, moves you to joy or sadness, induces moods of thoughtfulness or sensuous delight or serene contemplation. To some people—perhaps to you—it suggests stories, to others pictures. Or it may call forth associations—places or things that you remember—making you think of love, fear, strife, triumph, of a thousand tragedies and comedies. Or it may appeal to your intellect by its display of ingenuity and logic, interesting you in the working out of themes and the carrying out of a structural plan.

You will find that certain works attract you for one of the above reasons, other works for another reason, but most really enjoyable works for several reasons jointly. By talking with other people who love the same works, or in the course of your readings, you will discover that the reasons for loving any one work may be very different. Later you will discover that the same reasons or principles may lead people to enjoy works that are as widely different as, say, Mozart's and Bartòk's. You will discover that very few works are so beautiful that all music lovers agree in loving them unreservedly. I know no single human being whose taste in music is on all points similar to my own ; I no more expect to encounter one than I expect to find any two human beings who have the same taste in music, or the same taste in food, wine, or landscape.

All this should not discourage nor even bewilder you. Exactly the same thing happens in all arts. All beautiful music—that is, all music which the ' passionate few ' agree in considering beautiful—is not equally loved by all. If only we had the courage to say so, and the sense to acknowledge the difference between admiring and loving, between the tribute of the mind and the tribute of the soul, we should get on ever so much better with questions of art. I am trying to develop, not your capacity for admiring music, but your capacity for loving it.

You will understand how natural it is that one work should attract you chiefly by its emotional suggestiveness, another chiefly by its dramatic eloquence, a third by the sheer beauty of its proportions ; and that you should set greater store by certain of these elements of artistic appeal, whereas other people ascribe greater virtue to other elements.

Quite apart from the fact that the education of taste, on the whole, is—or should be—never-ending, and that a good many things besides taste pure and simple influence our musical preferences, it remains true that even the most experienced and unprejudiced of us are to some extent governed by pure and irreducible idiosyncrasies of taste. The advantages of education are that at least it enables us to progress up to the point where the irreducible part of our nature is reached—it is a very small part really, although its influence may be great—and then to realize how far this limits or determines our musical outlook and our capacity to enjoy music.

A point of crucial importance is that instinctive and educated tastes alike are often characterized by an overbalance in a certain direction, with results that may become disastrous. To know that our taste is affected by some kind of overbalance is really half the battle, because the knowledge, even if it does not lead us to react, serves as a warning. Few of us, if any, may hope to achieve perfect balance : but we all may hope to enrich and improve our instinctive taste.

Exactly as you have learnt to refrain from overrating the purely sensuous appeal of beautiful tone—not in deference to any æsthetic principle, real or alleged, but because you felt that it might stand in the way of greater and more certain and more lasting joys—you will learn not to overrate the things that attract you, and to enjoy things that left you cold. You will learn a good deal without ever asking yourself in the abstract whether certain tastes are ' better ' than others. Indeed, you should never ask yourself this question as a point of method or out of a sense of duty. For you cannot hope to find the answer before question and answer together come to you in a flash.

The next chapter will point out a few instances of musical tastes affected by overbalance in certain directions. But I must give you one forthwith so as to dispose of the interesting question of the sensuous appeal of music.

In music even of the most austere kind, there is an element of sensuous appeal—exactly as there is in the tone of a voice or instrument. It may be great or small ; it may depend upon design or upon colour, or both. It may also depend upon volume of sound. There is a far greater amount and variety of pure colour in Chopin's piano music than in Bach's and in Debussy's than in Chopin's. Volume of sound plays a more prominent part in Beethoven's piano music than in Mozart's or Bach's. Some people underrate the importance of these sensuous elements, others overrate it.

A curious instance of the latter tendency is to be found in the following passage of Berlioz's book, *A Travers Chants :*

' If one member of a big group of church singers gives out a simple theme, slow in tempo and not very interesting in itself, however beautiful his voice and artistic his singing, the effect will be poor ; but the same theme, repeated less artistically in *unison* by all, will assume an incredible majesty.'

This, although grossly overstated, is not altogether nonsense. But the moral is that overbalance of taste for volume of sound may lead to underrate music that does not cater for this particular form of taste. And indeed we find the same

Berlioz writing of Mozart's use of a solo trombone in his
Requiem :

' Poor Mozart, who is content with a single trombone—
when five hundred would have been hardly sufficient ! '

Berlioz's taste was characterized by an overbalance in
the direction of volume. He was for ever dreaming of giant
orchestras. This led him as a composer to achieve a number
of fine effects : but it certainly restricted his capacity for
enjoying music. He loved Beethoven's works deeply : but
it is doubtful whether he was capable of enjoying Beethoven's
piano and chamber music as deeply as he enjoyed his symphonies.

Conversely there have been people who found Wagner's
music too noisy and could not discover any quality in
it beyond the volume of sound. So that it is quite obvious
that overbalance of taste in any direction, be it for high
colour and volume or quietness, for simplicity or com-
plexity, for impressiveness or soberness, for elements of
familiarity or for elements of surprise, limits our capacity
for enjoyment. And it carries no compensating advantage
as does the education which restricts our enjoyment to the
music best capable of giving us great, sure, and lasting
pleasure.

CHAPTER VIII

THE TASTE FOR THE MUSIC

T H E other ways in which music can affect us pleasurably are by appealing to our emotions, stimulating our imagination, interesting our intellect, and suggesting associations of various kinds. Let us consider these one by one, beginning with the last—which happens to be the source of endless and disastrous misapprehension.

Suppose you enjoy a piece of music because it evokes visions and dreams of love, it may be for three distinct reasons : first, because the music itself directly arouses your emotions and stimulates your imagination in a certain direction ; secondly, because a title, or a ' programme ' appended to the music by its composer, or something written by a biographer or critic of the composer, informs you that the music owes its inspiration to thoughts of love or to a love-story ; or thirdly, because you remember hearing the piece at a time when you were in love.

If so you will easily realize that the reason why you like the piece may have nothing to do with your musical taste nor with music. The piece might be ten times worse and yet appeal to you as strongly ; and other music which you consider ten times better will never have that particular attraction for you.

I give this very crude instance in order to show what a number of things that have not the faintest relation to musical taste may influence and even determine our likes and dislikes.

It may be a surprise to you to learn that the information conveyed by titles and programmes and stories about what the composers did or thought when writing a certain work is equally misleading. The more attention you pay to it, the more obstacles in the way of your acquiring a discriminating musical taste.

You may think that I am simply flying in the face of facts, since very great musicians of all times have given titles and often programmes to some of their masterpieces, and since the soundest writers do not hesitate to refer to facts of Beethoven's, Schumann's, or Wagner's life when commenting on their works.

But this, after all, is the poorest of makeshifts when the object is to acquire insight into musical beauty. When you are told that you must 'try to see the man behind his music', you should be reminded in the same breath that—to quote Romain Rolland's words—' a few pages of a great composer's music will tell us more about his soul than his biographies and correspondence'. If you wish to go further into this point, Chapter V of my *Principles and Methods of Musical Criticism* may prove helpful to you.

But even so, you will perhaps ask, what about the titles and ' programmes ' supplied by the composers themselves ? I am not attempting to go into the reasons they had for doing so, nor to suggest that the practice is objectionable. What I wish to impress upon you is that titles and programmes, however legitimate, should not exercise the slightest influence upon your judgement. A good many people who devoutly believe that ' programme music ' is inferior to ' pure music ' will unhesitatingly condemn musical works as inferior simply because they are provided with a programme or title. The well-worn jibe : ' when will somebody write a " music symphony " ? ' has no other origin. One writer on musical appreciation disposes of Liszt's music simply by saying that ' Liszt's subjects are used to indicate individuals, ideas, or circumstances '—which, even if it were true, would leave the question of their musical beauty or ugliness untouched.

Other people incline to take the significance of a musical work for granted on the strength of its label. This is equally unwise : for it may blunt their power of discrimination.

You are not prepared to admit, I am sure, that the *Poème de l'Extase* or the *Pastoral Symphony*, which delight you, would delight you less if they were simply entitled *Symphonic Rhapsody* and *Symphony in F major*. But perhaps you feel that a title, or a programme, or maybe information as to the composer's intentions and frame of mind at the time of composing a work, may help you when you are in a quandary. It is precisely when you are in a quandary that such help is most dangerous. It will pay you to try to solve your doubts by safer and more direct means, although it may appear less easy. Understand that when you are looking at Leonardo's *Mona Lisa* you need not be told that it represents a beautiful, enigmatic woman. A very poor painting might bear the label 'Portrait of a Beautiful, Enigmatic Woman'. It would probably not deceive you one instant. It is open to any composer to invite you to believe that a work of his stands as a monument of rapturous inspiration simply by tacking on to it some such label as *Poème de l'Extase*. But whether it is or not the music alone can tell.

In other words, a title, a programme, a biographical fact can only enlighten us as to a composer's intentions or reasons for composing a work. It is his achievements only that matter. Unless you learn to judge achievements apart from intentions, your musical taste stands in great danger of never improving.

There are, it is true, excellent critics who aver that when listening to music written on the basis of a programme, such as Balakiref's *Tamara* or Strauss's *Don Quixote* or Elgar's *Falstaff*, you derive additional pleasure from knowing both the programme and the music. This I do not wish to deny any more than I should wish to deny the additional pleasure you derive from the tune you heard when you were in love, or from appraising the skill with which a composer suggests the tramp of camels or the last gurgle of Till on the gallows. My only point is that such things, and perhaps many others, may be there, but cannot be added any more than a foot and a pound and a pint. But, of course, if the notion of tramping camels may play a part in the inspiration of music so utterly lovely as Borodin's *The Steppes of Central Asia*, and that of the fatal drop play a part in music so entertaining as Strauss's *Till Eulenspiegel*, then music lovers may well be as favourably disposed towards programme music as towards pure music.

You will have realized, I hope, that I am not dealing with the matter from the point of view of abstract philosophy. I couldn't, even if I wanted to, because there are many ' programmatic ' works which I love as deeply, and indeed love exactly in the same way, as I love the ' pure ' music I love best. I am only telling you that so long as you depend upon collateral information of any kind, your enjoyment of music will remain precarious.

Now, I expect, you fully understand why, in my third chapter, I urged you to begin with instrumental music. I did not wish to lure you away from song and opera any more than I now wish to lure you away from programme music ; I only wish to guide you straightaway towards what must be your ultimate object : the acquisition of that clear-sightedness, discipline, and freedom of outlook which will enable you to judge and enjoy musical works on their purely musical merits.

It is often said that musical works are better appreciated when 'seen in their historical perspective ', that is, considered with reference to the conditions under which they came into being. The truth is, that knowledge of this kind is satisfying and desirable as knowledge—all knowledge is— but has no bearing whatever on artistic enjoyment.

The historical method is useful to students because musical forms began by being very simple, and gradually grew more complex. When you wish to learn to analyse works, it is advisable to start with Mozart's or Haydn's symphonies before you tackle Beethoven's or Brahms's, or Franck's one symphony. But remember that beauty is a quality which soars high above conditions of time, place, and circumstance. When you look at a chair or a vase or a picture or a cathedral, you do not feel the need to ' see them in their historical perspective ' before deciding whether they are beautiful or not. You would, very sensibly, pooh-pooh the suggestion that to know the name of the cabinet-maker or potter or architect or painter might influence your appraisement of what is standing before you. But with regard to music, assertions of this kind are usually allowed to pass unchallenged.

Let us speedily clear up all these points. It is quite true that if you know a musical work to be by a composer whose music has impressed you favourably, you start by expecting this work to be worthy of attention. But this applies only until you are acquainted with the work itself. If you are at all in earnest, you will devote the same unprejudiced attention to all works that are new to you, whatever their authorship.

When you are told that it may help you to know that music you hear is Chinese, or sixteenth century, you are not to understand that its date or place of origin affect its beauty or ugliness. But the Chinese—or the sixteenth century—conception of beauty and sense of proportion and artistic fitness may comprise elements lacking in yours as well as lack elements which yours may comprise. Therefore, to acquire experience of the Chinese outlook or of the sixteenth-century outlook, even if it does not lead you to enjoy Chinese music or sixteenth-century music, will contribute to the education of your twentieth-century European taste and make you readier and better qualified to enjoy music of any country or century.

It is often pointed out that the conditions under which Haydn wrote—his duty was to provide music suited to the requirements of an eighteenth-century court and aristocracy—made it imperative for him to conform to a certain etiquette and fashion, exactly as he had to wear a wig and ruffles :

but that despite its conventional apparel, his music is live and genuine and instinct with fantasy and eloquence. To call your attention to these points in order to invite you, if need be, to look beneath the surface may be useful : but it is only when you have actually felt how original and telling Haydn's music is that the result is achieved. So long as you have not, reference to the conditions under which Haydn wrote will mean as little to you as the assertion uttered by a young composer of to-day that 'the listnessness of to-day's audiences makes it imperative that each bar of music should jigger and jolt them'. There may be beauty within the polite scheme of court music and within the rude scheme of jiggering and jolting. But if there is none, then no amount of explanation will make up for it. The best taste, the taste that makes for swiftest and surest enjoyment of what is enjoyable, is the taste that goes straight for the music. How you acquire it does not matter much, but it is desirable for you to acquire it as soon as possible. My one quarrel with some of the courses advocated in books on Appreciation is that instead of inviting you to face the main issue forthwith, they carry you round and round until, mayhap, looking for the accessory fact leads you to lose sight of the essential.

You feel, I know, that I am continually talking of the essential and never getting any nearer to it. All these remarks and precautions of mine are trying your patience sorely. A friend and colleague of mine has said, or nearly, that my attitude in my *Principles and Methods of Musical Criticism* reminded him of that of the mother who said to the governess : ' Miss Brown, pray see what the children are doing and tell them they mustn't ! '

When he reads this book he will give me up as hopeless. I cannot help it. I warned you that I was not going to present you with a set of recipes for telling good music from bad. There is no such thing. The best I can do is to remove one by one all the traps in your way and show you a good course. Have a little more patience. I cannot invite you to skip any of this part, as I did the two chapters on theory. There are one or two more traps to dispose of.

The next is the trap of emotion. Here I can see you losing all patience and asking indignantly : ' What *is* the fellow talking about ? Is not emotion the supreme end of art ? ' And my reply is : ' Yes, undoubtedly : but there are many degrees and kinds of emotion, and you must learn to beware of the overbalance of emotion, the indulgence in the wrong kind of emotion, that will narrow your musical outlook instead of broadening it '.

I have already warned you against this danger by warning you against associations—although the analogy is very loose, it will serve our present purely practical purpose.

Remember my imaginary instance of the time when, being in love, you heard a piece of music which thenceforth acquired a special significance for you. Perhaps if you heard it for the first time now, it would strike you as merely maudlin, high-falutin', or empty. But when you heard it you were in an over-emotional condition. Not only the poorest music, but the poorest picture or poem or play or magazine story capable of pandering to your appetite for emotion would have stirred you. It was the emotions that mattered to you, not the music. In short, your condition was the very reverse of that which might make for the appreciation of musical beauty.

Among the masterpieces of music, none is more deeply charged with emotion than the first movement of Beethoven's Fifth Symphony. No music lover could listen to it without a thrill. But the fact that Beethoven once said of its main motive : ' Thus does Fate knock at our door ' has led many people to take a highly sentimental and melodramatic view of this admirable music. One adviser on Musical Appreciation has written :

' If, when hearing this first movement, we obtain from its main theme merely the sense of something impetuous, and do not hear the hammerstrokes of Fate knocking at

Beethoven's door and saying " you shall suffer—suffer—suffer—you shall be deaf as a stone—you shall never know domestic joys " . . . we miss much that it is a thousand pities to miss.'

Taken at its face value, this notion leads to preposterous interpretations such as this one, which I found in a German periodical :

' Fate does not knock : it strikes man to the ground. Whenever the panting victim struggles to arise (e.g. bars 33-43) he is ruthlessly thrown down again (bars 43-56). The second theme, with its two downward fifths, outbids the first. Thus does Fate grind its heel on man's neck and press it hard on the ground (the long-sustained deep B flat), while man begs for mercy.'

This instance of overbidding is more instructive, I think, than any explanations could be. Could any attitude be more unworthy of fine music ? The same kind of yarns might be spun, the same kind of unbalanced excitement might arise, on the strength of a piece beginning with loud bangs on the bass drum and continuing with woodwinds realistically moaning and trombones threatening and a thousand similar things. The more you allow such considerations to invade the foreground, the less able you will be to appraise the quality of the music. This is what Mr. W. J. Turner means when, in his book *Music and Life*, he says, quite bluntly : ' The emotional listener misses everything that distinguishes music from the other arts'. And I urge you to meditate these words from Mr. Greening Lamborn's *Rudiments of Criticism :* they apply to music as truly as to poetry :

' Emotion is not poetry, but the cause of poetry ; and emotional expression is only poetry when it takes a beautiful form. An uncritical susceptibility to mere sentiment is more dangerous than a craving for strong drink.'

Last in my catalogue of traps comes the trap of intellectual enjoyment. I make no apology for springing this declaration on you. By this time you probably feel that nothing coming from me could surprise you.

But in point of fact I can prove that this trap exists simply by quoting Sir Henry Hadow's declaration that ' Hummel and Czerny copied Beethoven's design but left the poetry out '. So that now I am just giving its full name to an obvious thing. The difference between a mere copy (that is, a mechanically planned and carried-out piece of music) and an inspired work are not within ken of the analysing and reasoning mind. They cannot be demonstrated nor even relevantly described. They can only be felt. This important distinction is dealt with more fully in the fourth chapter of my *Principles and Methods of Musical Criticism* (Oxford University Press).

The time has now come to point out that the enjoyment of skill is essentially intellectual ; it is the result of a conscious or unconscious operation of the mind, nothing more. The story about the actor and the footlights told on p. 22 illustrates this point well. Probably the actor's skill was as strikingly demonstrated in this little display as it might have been in the interpretation of the finest poetry. The listeners were comparing in their minds his materials and what he was able to do with them—exactly as certain listeners may be impressed by the fact that a composer gets hold of a poor tune and does fifty ingenious and unexpected things with it.

This, of course, is confusing the means with the end. Another illustration may make the point clearer. Given a piece of sculpture, it may be of interest to know whether it was made with no help but that of a knife, or with a complete set of the best tools. The knowledge that it was made with a knife may lend zest to our enjoyment by increasing our admiration for the maker's skill. And how much more thrilling it would be to learn that the only tool used was the convict's traditional rusty nail ! But when all is said and done, all such considerations leave the question of the sculpture's beauty untouched.

F

I am not alleging that conscious intellectual enjoyment should be excluded from your scheme. This would be as foolish as it would be to say that composers do not bring their intellect to bear upon their work as well as all his other faculties. Indeed, all fine music, be it simple or intricate, is a treat to the intellect as well as to the emotions and imagination. It is only the taste which places intellectual enjoyment first, and allows it to encroach unduly, that is by so much the poorer, since it may remain incapable of discriminating between genuine artistic achievement and mechanical semblance.

I have done at last with my cautions, and reached the point when I must talk of the essential—which, for the true enjoyment of music, the ideal enjoyment what is governed and limited by no habits and no routine, is exactly the same as for the creation of fine music: it is imagination.

I can say very little about it. Imagination is utterly inexplicable. But I know, and everybody knows, that in most of you it exists. Whether in any one of you it is slow or swift, temperate or wayward, free or beset by habits, whether it stands in need of encouragement and guidance, I could only tell if I stood face to face with you and questioned you and heard what you have to say of music of various kinds. But I shall try to show you how to find that out for yourselves.

As I told you before, I cannot make things clear by appealing to your experiences outside music. It is music, and music only, that must tell its own tale.

On p. 87 are a few examples of things which all music lovers will probably agree in considering as utterly lovely; six of melodies, one of harmony.

I can tell you nothing relevant of them except that they are lovely, trusting that you will feel their loveliness. I can tell you anything you please about them except the exact reasons why they are so lovely. And what applies to brief patterns such as these is equally true of musical works con-

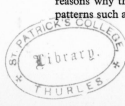

sidered as wholes. They must appeal to the imagination first and last or fall short in their appeal.

It is wonderful indeed to see how a Bach fugue, a Mozart or Beethoven symphony are constructed, to feel and observe how repetitions and imitations and developments and contrasts ' work towards a divinely preappointed end '. But it is impossible to explain how and why they do it, exactly as it is impossible to explain how each note works towards a divinely preappointed end within the scheme of one melodic or harmonic pattern. Music is a whole.

In order to show you how to acknowledge excellence of form (which is the same thing as continuity of interest), I can only do the same as I did when pointing to beauty in melody and harmony : I can only call your attention to a few clear, unquestionable examples of beauty of form, and trust that your experiences with these examples will give you something for you to build upon. Countless instances, of course, could be adduced from Bach, Haydn, Mozart, and Beethoven alone. An excellent start might be made with Bach's 48 Preludes and Fugues, Mozart's G Minor Symphony, Beethoven's *Coriolanus* Overture, Wagner's *Lohengrin* Prelude and *Siegfried Idyll*, and Debussy's *Prélude à l'Après Midi d'un Faune*. I select simple instances on purpose, and quite regardless of the question whether their form has a recognized label in current scholastic nomenclature or not.

Later, you will perhaps study questions of form with the help of some book. This will be an excellent thing to do. Any standard book on form will prove useful. I have seen a certain piece by Schumann described as an example of ' binary ' form in one book and as an example of ' ternary ' form in another. I have also seen a book that described as belonging to the second theme in a Beethoven symphony a pattern which another book described as belonging to the first theme. All this does not matter in the least. I would as gladly put into your hands the books that say the one thing as those that say the other thing, because all happen to be excellent for the purpose of teaching you how to analyse music. By the time you feel impelled to read them, you will probably have learnt never to believe that the analysis which they give are intended to show you why the music thus analysed is beautiful. And if you come across statements such as : ' This work is in no duly recognized and labelled form ; it lacks this or that customary landmark (e.g. it does not end in the key in which it began)—therefore its form is bad ', you will not consider them as conclusive in themselves : for you will have acquired, at least partly, the experience which will enable you to perceive the essential, and not the obvious only.

CHAPTER IX

EXPERIENCE

W H E N we are told that X—— or Z—— copied A—— or B——'s design but left out the poetry, we may wonder how far any one of us would be aware that X—— or Z——'s music lacks poetry but for comparative experience. Supposing the music of A—— and B—— and of all composers who poured genuine poetry into the forms which X—— and Z—— are alleged to have copied mechanically had vanished, would we still realize the poor quality of X—— and Z——'s music ? This is an interesting point for philosophers ; but it does not interest you just now, since fortunately there is plenty of music from which you may derive comparative experience.

I mention comparison in the same breath as experience because the two are inseparable. To acquire experience, you must not only go through plenty of experiences—that is, hear plenty of music of all kinds—but compare your experiences with one another and with those of other people. This is the whole secret.

Naturally you will find it most instructive to start by comparing your experiences of the great classics with those which have been recorded for your benefit by keen music lovers and able judges of music. Having listened to a Beethoven symphony or a Mozart quartet, and retaining from the experience a strong but perhaps not altogether clear impression, you will find analytical comments useful for the simple reason that they suggest means of reducing your impressions to some sort of order.

You may wish to read these, as a precautionary measure, before you hear the music. My advice is : do so then, provided they refer to works which you are about to play or to have played for you or are sure to have an early chance of hearing more than once. But as a rule, during the first stages of your education, avoid doing so if it is likely that some time may elapse before you hear the work again. Above all things do not read notices while listening. The programme you bought may seem replete with alluring information. Resist the temptation, and stick it into your pocket before the music starts.

When listening to a Shakespeare play you would not care to have somebody diverting your attention by telling you : ' Now, isn't this beautiful ? ' or ' here we have six metaphors in succession, all equally relevant and impressive', or ' look out for the admirable reference to the perfumes of Arabia.' You wish to concentrate, not to scatter your attention. You do not want, instead of listening, to keep watching for that re-entry of the clarinet or that combination of motives No. 3 and No. 17, which are so alluringly described. All this, and a good deal besides, may and should find its proper place in your exercises in ear and memory training. What you must do when listening to music is just to listen, thus gradually acquiring experiences which you may afterwards compare with those of which you read descriptions, and noticing things which you may afterwards compare with the technical descriptions in the programme notice or in your books.

It is even more instructive to compare one musical work with another. And most instructive of all is comparison between good works and bad.

Perhaps you feel that now you have really caught me in the act of self-contradiction. But I am not about to lay down a law as to good music and bad. I simply mean that it will be convenient for you to start by comparing certain more or less generally recognized examples of ' good ' music with certain more or less generally recognized examples of ' bad '. The labels are only temporary. You may interchange them or tear them off, if you wish, as soon as your comparison is effected. A very few may suffice to enlighten you, or many will prove needful: you may rest assured that every single one of them will be helpful. Your ultimate object is not merely to know your own mind, but to feel sure that you know it as well as possible and have done your utmost to test it.

When an honest and wise critic tells you things such as : ' A—— and B—— copied X——'s design but left out the poetry ' he is not asking you to take things on trust : he is enabling and actually inviting you to look and see for yourselves. Consider how very much more useful to you his way of putting things is that the bare assertion ' there is no poetry in A——'s or B——'s music ' would have been. If, after having grown familiar with X——'s music, you continue to feel that there is plenty of poetry in A——'s or B——'s, you will still be able to tell yourself, quite rightly, that your enjoyment of their music was increased by comparative experience.

The one drawback of experience is that it begets habits. I have already warned you that, however much we enjoy our habits, habits sometimes set a limit to our capacity for artistic enjoyment, because they predispose us against all that lies outside their scope.

Hadow, in his *Studies in Modern Music*, recalls the story of a visitor to Constable's studio who said to the painter : ' Your new landscape is all very well : but where are you going to put your brown tree ? ' A landscape without a brown tree did not come within this visitor's experiences of paintings, therefore the brown tree had become a matter of habit to him ; thence to believe that the presence of a brown tree is an inevitable law is but one step. The critic who described Balakiref's beautiful tone-poem *Tamara* as formless ' because it does not end in the key in which it begins ' was simply looking for *his* brown tree. Very foolishly, a certain writer on Appreciation tells his readers that ' the great classics have left models for composers to copy '. Taken literally, this assertion would mean that the ' brown tree ' notion is to endure for ever.

The point is so vital that I feel I must illustrate it further, selecting my instance, this time, from laws or habits that once seemed imperative in dramatic art. At a very early date, it was observed that if a play was founded on one definite event only, taking place at one spot and in the course of one single day, unity and clarity of structure were easily achieved by the playwright and easily realized by the spectator. Hence the ' law of the three unities ' came into being. The French dramatists of the seventeenth century and their public accepted this law literally. It is instructive to see how earnestly questions such as whether two rooms in one palace may be considered as one spot, or whether the action of a certain play can really take place in less than a day and a quarter were debated, and the play pronounced well-constructed or not according to the reply on such points. Even at a much later date, French criticism considered Shakespeare's plays as altogether formless, without further inquiry, because to them the rule of the three unities (by that time a mere matter of local convention or habit) was a permanent, inviolable law.

It is certainly not easy to determine exactly when an alleged musical law becomes a mere matter of habit. The safest course for beginners is to ignore all arguments based on the alleged existence or non-existence of this law or that. Wordsworth has written : ' Every great and original artist, in proportion as he is great and original, must himself create the taste by which he is to be relished ; he must teach the art by which he is to be seen.' This splendid axiom, which everybody concerned with artistic education should know by heart and constantly remember, means that the only cure against habit is more experience. If from many great and original artists in turn you learn the art by which each of them is to be seen, you will acquire, not set habits, but that discriminating, keen responsiveness and thorough flexibility which I had in view when urging you never to take anything for granted.

When you are comparing works for the purpose of acquiring insight into the differences between ' good ' and ' bad ', be careful to compare works whose scope, aims, and idiosyncrasies are as similar as possible. As a beginner, you will learn nothing by comparing a bad fugue with a good set of variations, or a good eighteenth-century quartet with a bad one in the style of Debussy or of some later innovator.

The question whether certain orders of music fulfil a better, loftier purpose than certain others need not detain you. A wedding march certainly fulfils a worthier purpose than a drinking song : but what you want is to be able to tell a musically good wedding march from a musically bad wedding march, and a musically good drinking song from a musically bad drinking song.

Here I see no objection to your comparing songs with one another, provided you understand that a song to words dealing with the majesty of the universe or the ecstasy of love is not necessarily better, as music, than one dealing with the village simpleton's feelings (Mussorgsky's *Savishna*) or the antics of a guinea-hen (Ravel's *La Pintade*), exactly as Strauss's *Heldenleben* is not necessarily better music than his *Merry Pranks of Till Eulenspiegel*.

Special interest attaches, of course, to comparisons between settings of one text by various composers. A classical instance is Goethe's poem *Wer nie sein Brot mit Tränen ass*, set to music by Schubert, Löwe, Liszt (twice), and Hugo Wolf.

As regards instrumental music, you might do worse than start by comparing instances of variation form—a form so simple that you will be able forthwith to devote your attention to musical substance without bothering about points of structure. Among the finest instances available I shall name Bach's Goldberg Variations, Beethoven's Diabelli Variations, the slow movements of Beethoven's string quar-

tets op. 127, 131, and 132, and Schumann's Symphonic
Studies, op. 13. This is quite enough to get on with. After
comparing them with one another, you will perhaps wish to
pass to a comparison between good variations and bad.
As instances of empty and tedious variations, almost any
musician would at once suggest something from the output of
Dussek or Czerny. If you feel that it is unfair to compare
Dussek or Czerny's music with the aforenamed masterpieces, you might take as the other term of your comparison
the lovely variations in the Adagio of Haydn's Sonata in E
flat, op. 78, which are nearer at least in outward characteristics.

But I should not like you to rest content with comparisons
between signal examples of acknowledged perfection and
music which most music lovers consider as unworthy of
the slightest attention. As soon as possible, start comparing
examples of the great masters at their best with examples
that show them not quite at their best. After studying the
admirable variations in the final section of Beethoven's pianoforte sonata op. 109, you might compare them with the
variations in the slow movement of his ' Kreutzer ' Sonata
for violin and pianoforte. This ought to enable you to realize
why the latter are not usually numbered among his finest
achievements. You will feel that there is something per-
functory in the way in which the theme is varied, and that
the movement, as a whole, is not so full of meat as the set of
variations in the sonata op. 109. A comparison with, at the
other end, a set of variations by a poor composer will prove
equally instructive.

When you start comparing not only the substance but the
form of works, you must again observe precautions : for
musical form is not really separable from musical substance.
If, when comparing works as different in form as Beethoven's
Coriolanus Overture, Wagner's *Siegfried Idyll*, Debussy's
Prélude à l'Après Midi d'un Faune and Borodin's *Steppes of
Central Asia* you feel that in all of them the form is perfect

because, as Mr. Ernest Newman puts it, ' good form is that in which not one note is superfluous and each fragment works towards a divinely preappointed end ', you are well on the way to learn all that there is to learn about form.

Later on you will, of course, study and compare forms as illustrated in works such as Beethoven's sonatas—for which purpose a book such as Forbes Milne's *Beethoven* (Oxford University Press) will prove useful.

Then will come comparison between good and less good. Supposing that as an instance of the less good I suggest a sonata by Grieg. In order to make you feel that the suggestion is justified, two courses are open. I can ask you to compare this sonata with Grieg's short piano pieces, those delightful little lyrics in which each note certainly works towards ' a divinely preappointed end ', and hope that you will realize that the sonata (any of the five Grieg has written) is different, rambling, loose, marred by repetitions which do not serve a definite purpose such as is served, for instance, by the repetitions in Grieg's *In the Hall of the Mountain King*. Or I can try a more scientific method, and invite you to compare the Grieg sonata with, say Beethoven's op. 57 (the ' Appassionata '), whose unity of structure is as easy to demonstrate in terms of technique as it is easy to feel.

The range of comparisons I might suggest is endless. But I have room for one more indication only. I wish you to learn to discriminate between sincerity of emotion (or purpose) and genuineness of expression (or achievement). The trouble is that I can think of no instance suitable for introduction in this booklet. To quote one would be to make a point of pure criticism, and my policy here is one of broad advice only—I have almost overstepped it already, while speaking of Grieg.

Read in Mr. Greening Lamborn's *Rudiments of Criticism*, pages 15 to 17, what he has to say of the comparison between Eliza Cook's verses on ' The Old Armchair ' and ten lines on a similar subject by Cowper. He tries to show that in the former ' the form of emotional expression does not convey the real emotion, and that those who fancy themselves "moved" by it are from laziness or carelessness taking the shadow for the substance and deluding themselves with mere words '. He makes a very good case for this view, not only because he can quote both examples in full, but because it is easier to explain, and easier to understand, why descriptions such as ' mere jingles ', ' vagueness and indefiniteness ', and so on, are true with regard to words than it would be to explain why they are true with regard to music. Yet all music lovers feel quite definitely whether the music they hear is or not ' a mere jingle ' or ' vague and indefinite '. Experience will lead you to feel it too.

The characteristics of a composer's incapacity to find the true emotional expression are that he borrows ready-made modes of expression, and generally exaggerates them. Drawing-room ballads of the ancient type are excellent instances. With regard to less obvious cases, I can only say this much : wishing to express some emotion for which he cannot create a genuine expression, the incapable or inexperienced composer will do something very similar to what a bad writer, intent on expressing the splendours of mercy and remembering Shakespeare might do, starting with ' The most rare and sublime quality of . .   ' or ' Mercy, mercy, most heavenly mercy, thy quality is never, never. . . . .' In the course of your readings on music, you will surely encounter denunciations of composers alleged to have committed similarly atrocious misdemeanours. Select the works thus pilloried for comparison with works which you love and know to be thought highly of by music lovers. Here I must finally leave you to your own resources. I have but one more task to fulfil, and that is to give you a short list of the works which you should try to know as soon as possible.

One more bit of advice is necessary. Read now, if you have not read it before, the opening essay in the first volume of Sir Henry Hadow's *Studies in Modern Music*, in which the

main characteristics of beauty in music are clearly defined. Nothing could assist you better in the task of 'arranging your emotions' and obtaining a glimpse of the reasons experienced music lovers have for describing works as beautiful or the reverse.

CHAPTER X

A FIRST LIST OF MUSIC

M Y aim is to mention, within the briefest possible compass, representative examples of as many different types of music as possible. This list is not intended to provide you with anything more than a temporary framework and guide.

I have restricted myself—this time merely for the sake of brevity—to instrumental music. I remind you of what I said of Wagner's music on p. 16, and call your attention to the fact that there is at least one great composer who cannot be adequately known except through his songs and dramatic music : Mussorgsky. Therefore let his *Boris Godunof* and his songs (published by Bessel) be added to the list.

I should have made it shorter but for the reason that I do not know which music will first stimulate your imagination. Mr. Rorke in his *Musical Pilgrim's Progress* mentions seventeen composers in all, and of these seventeen less than half played a part in his initiation.

The one thing that can be safely foretold is that a great proportion of the music mentioned hereafter will appeal to you very soon.

The list will perhaps be found by you not to include certain works which you enjoy or have heard described as enjoyable. But remember that it is not intended to stand instead of that which you will eventually compile for yourselves.

It should not be taken as representing my own preferences. It contains things which I included very much against my own feeling, but in deference to the feelings of a majority of experienced music lovers. On the other hand, whenever I was satisfied that sufficient disagreement to justify my doing so existed among experienced music lovers as to the value of certain works, I decided in favour of their inclusion or exclusion according to my own feeling as to the probable value of these works for the purpose of educating your taste. Hence, for instance, the deliberate omission of Scriabin.

I have given more particulars about modern music than about classical music, because this is where guidance is most needful to you and most difficult to get. But to provide guidance in a book such as this one remains a delicate matter. It is easy enough to pick out a number of composers whose music stands for something new and definite, and has been found worthy of attention by people who obviously belong to the 'passionate few'. Yet, after careful consideration, I decided not to attempt to cover the ground fully in this case any more than in that of the classics.

The first part of the list contains original piano works which you should not only hear at concerts, but play yourselves or get played to you by friends. I have attempted no hard and fast distinction between ' easy ' and difficult things ; but a few easy, or comparatively easy pieces, are marked E.

A second part contains works which you should try to hear played in their original form, but also play or hear played by others in piano transcriptions. A piano-player may also be brought into requisition for studying most of the works and transcriptions referred to in both these parts.

A third part contains works which you will have to hear played in their original form only, transcriptions being unavailable or, if they exist, unsatisfactory.

J S. Bach	This name naturally heads the list. Hear and play as much of Bach's music as ever you can, from the small Inventions to the Forty-Eight Preludes and Fugues (of which the Harold Brooke's Edition (Novello) and Prof. Tovey's (for the Associated Board) are in all respects most commendable), the Suites, the Partitas, etc. The better you know these, the more you will be struck with their eloquence and imaginativeness.
English Virginalists Couperin Rameau Scarlatti C.P.E.Bach	Any standard edition of this delightful keyboard music will do.
Beethoven Schubert Schumann Chopin	These four deserve your utmost attention. You should know all their output. Any standard British or Continental edition will do.
César Franck	Wrote only two works for piano, but both are of paramount significance: Prélude, Choral, et Fugue Prélude, Aria, et Finale *Enoch Hamelle*

Liszt	Has written a surprising amount of surprisingly bad music (some of which is far more widely known than his fine music), but also some of the very finest things in the musical output of the nineteenth century. The original piano works of his that I recommend here are :	
	Années de Pélerinage—3 books	Schott
	Two Legends	
	Sonata	Breitkopf
	Grandes Etudes d'exécution transcendante.	„
	Harmonies Poétiques et Religieuses.	
Grieg	Most typical of his charming genius are the Lyrical Pieces Op. 3, 12, 43, 47, 54, 57, 62, 65.	Peters
	Ballade	
Borodin	His only original compositions for piano are a Petite Suite (E) and a Scherzo; they are well worth knowing.	Augener
Balakiref	Most characteristic among his piano works is the beautiful Fantasy *Islamey*	Jurgenson
Chabrier	Dix Pièces Pittoresques	Enoch
	Bourrée Fantasque	„

G

Debussy	Préludes (two books)	Durand
	Estampes	,,
	Images	,,
Ravel	Miroirs	Eschig
	Gaspard de la Nuit	Durand
	Sonatine (E)	,,
Koechlin	Petites Pièces and Pièces Faciles (E)	Senart
	Sonatines (E)	Mathot

These easy pieces are particularly enjoyable and well worth studying.

	Paysages et Marines	,,
	Sonatines (duet)	Oxford University Press
Bax	Piano Sonatas	Murdoch
	Mediterranean	,,
John Ireland	London Pieces	Augener's
	The Darkened Valley	,,
	Merry Andrew	Ascherberg
Bartòk	Four books of easy pieces :	
	Pro Déti and A *Gyrmekeknek*	Rozsnyai
	Quatre Nénies	Universal Ed.
	Sonatine (E)	,,
	Dix Pièces Faciles (E)	Rozsnyai

All these will be found to constitute the best possible introduction to contemporary music.

| Albeniz | Iberia, 12 pieces | Rouart |
| de Falla | Four Spanish Dances | Eschig |

SECOND PART

J. S. Bach	Transcription of Six Organ Fugues by Liszt	Peters
Haydn Mozart Beethoven	Quartets, concertos and symphonies of these three masters exist arranged for solo or duet, and should occupy a place of honour in your musical library. Any standard edition will do.	
Schubert	' Unfinished ' Symphony Posthumous Quartet in D	
Mendelssohn	' Italian ' and ' Scotch ' symphonies Overtures : A Midsummer Night's Dream The Hebrides Melusine	
Weber	Freyschütz Overture	
Schumann Brahms	First and Fourth Symphonies Manfred Overture Piano Concerto Symphonies	
Liszt	Faust Symphony Dante Symphony These two works are of paramount significance. It is all the more desirable that you should learn to know them in transcriptions for the reason that	Schuberth Breitkopf and Härtel

they are hardly ever performed
in this country
Variations on a theme of Bach

Borodin	Two symphonies (duet)	Bessel
	Unfinished symphony (duet, E)	Belaief
	Two String Quartets (duet)	,,
	The Steppes of Central Asia (E)	,,
	All these make most delight-	
	ful duet-playing	
Balakiref	Tamara (duet)	Jurgenson
Rimsky	Antar, symphonic suite (duet)	Belaief
Korsakof	Schéhérazade do.	,,
	Sadko, tone poem (duet)	,,
Glazunof	Tone poems, Stenka Râzin (duet)	,,
	Oriental Rhapsody (duet)	,,
	Second and Third Symphonies	,,
	(duet)	
Dvořàk	Symphonies	
Smetana	Tone poems, *Mein Vaterland*	Urbanék
	Quartet, *Aus Meinem leben*	,,
Stravinsky	Petrushka (ballet)	Kussevitsky
	Le Sacre du Printemps (ballet)	,,
Sibelius	Tone poem, Finlandia	Breitkopf and
	Tone poem, Tuonela's Swan	Härtel
	Fourth and Fifth Symphonies	
Franck	Symphony	Hamelle
	String Quartet	,,
	Three Organ Chorales	Durand

Saint Saens	Tone Poems, *Phaéton, La Jeunesse d'Hercule, le Rouet d'Omphale*	Durand
V. d'Indy	Symphonie sur un Chant Montagnard Francais	Hamelle
	Trilogy *Wallenstein*	Durand
Dukas	L'Apprenti Sorcier	Durand
	La Péri	
Debussy	Prélude à l'Aprés-Midi d'un Faune	Jobert
	Trois Nocturnes	,,
Ravel	Daphnis et Chloé (ballet)	Durand
Elgar	First and Second Symphonies	Novello
	Tone Poem, *Falstaff*	,,
Bax	Moy Mell	Murdoch
Delius	Appalachia	Universal Edition
	Dance Rhapsody, No. 1	Edition
	Dance Rhapsody, No. 2	Augener
Vaughan Williams	London Symphony	Stainer and Bell
Holst	Planets	Curwen
	St. Paul's Suite	

THIRD PART

Bach	Violin Sonatas, Concertos, and other chamber music works	
Handel	Chamber Sonatas, Concertos, etc.	
Mozart	Quintets (strings, string and horn, clarinet)	
Beethoven	Trio, op. 97	
Schumann	Piano Quintet First Piano Trio	
Brahms	String Quintets, op. 88 and 111 Quintet with clarinet, op. 115 Piano Trio, op. 101	
Franck	Piano Quintet Violin Sonata	Hamelle ,,
Fauré	Second Piano Quartet Piano Quintets	,, Schirmer Durand
Florent Schmitt	Piano Quintet	Mathot
Schönberg	Sextet *Verklärte Nacht*	Universal Edition
Kodaly	String Quartets Serenade for two violins and viola Duet for violin and cello	Universal Edition ,,
Bartòk	String Quartets	,,

EXAMPLES

(see pages 66 and 67)

Ex.1   Bach, Toccata from First Partita

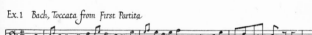

Ex.2   Bach, The '48' Book I, Fugue 21
Allegretto

Ex. 3   Beethoven, String Quartet, Op. 135
Lento assai

Ex. 4   Franck, String Quartet
Larghetto

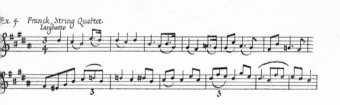

Ex. 5   Mussorgsky, Boris Godunof

Ex. 6   Vincent d'Indy, Fervaal

Ex. 7   Wagner, The Valkyrie